first
IMPRESSIONS

More than 100 elegant and delicious recipes to start the meal

first
IMPRESSIONS

CONSULTANT EDITOR: CHRISTINE INGRAM

southwater

This edition published by Southwater

Southwater is an imprint of
Anness Publishing Limited
Hermes House
88–89 Blackfriars Road
London SE1 8HA
tel. 020 7401 2077
fax. 020 7633 9499

Distributed in the UK by
The Manning Partnership
251–253 London Road East
Batheaston
Bath BA1 7RL
tel. 01225 852 727
fax. 01225 852 852

Distributed in the USA by
Anness Publishing Inc.
27 West 20th Street
Suite 504
New York, NY 10011
tel. 212 807 6739
fax. 212 807 6813

Distributed in Australia by
Sandstone Publishing
Unit 1, 360 Norton Street
Leichhardt
New South Wales 2040
tel. 02 9560 7888
fax. 02 9560 7488

© 2001 Anness Publishing Limited

1 3 5 7 9 10 8 6 4 2

Previously published as *Appetizers, Starters & Hors d'oeuvres*

Publisher: Joanna Lorenz
Managing Editor: Judith Simons
Editor: Charlotte Berman
Designer: Bill Mason, Jane Coney
Production Controller: Yolande Denny
Recipes: Catherine Atkinson, Alex Barker, Steve Baxter, Angela Boggiano, Carla Capalbo, Kit Chan, Jacqueline Clarke,
Maxine Clarke, Andi Cleverley, Roz Denny, Joanne Farrow, Rafi Fernandez, Silvano Franco, Christine France, Sarah Gates,
Shirley Gill, Nicola Graimes, Rosamund Grant, Carole Handslip, Deh-Ta Hsing, Peter Jordan, Elisabeth Lambert Ortiz,
Ruby Le Bois, Clare Lewis, Sara Lewis, Leslie Mackley, Norma MacMillan, Sally Mansfield, Sue Maggs, Sallie Morris, Jenny Stacey,
Liz Trigg, Hilaire Walden, Laura Washburn, Steven Wheeler, Kate Whiteman, Elizabeth Wolf-Cohen, Jenni Wright
Photography: Karl Adamson, Edward Allwright, Steve Baxter, James Duncan, John Freeman, Ian Garlick, Michelle Garrett,
Peter Henley, John Heseltine, Janine Hosegood, Amanda Heywood, David Jordan, Maria Kelly, Dave King, Don Last,
William Lingwood, Patrick McLeavey, Michael Michaels, Thomas Odulate, Sam Stowell

NOTES

For all recipes, quantities are given in both metric and imperial measures and,
where appropriate, measures are also given in standard cups and spoons.
Follow one set, but not a mixture, because they are not interchangeable.

Standard spoon and cup measurements are level.

1 tsp = 5ml, 1 tbsp = 15ml, 1 cup = 250ml/8fl oz

Australian standard tablespoons are 20ml. Australian readers should use 3 tsp
in place of 1 tbsp for measuring small quantities of gelatine, cornflour, salt etc.

Medium eggs should be used unless otherwise stated.

Contents

6   *Introduction*

8   *Soups*

36   *Pâtés, Terrines & Soufflés*

58   *Pastries, Tartlets & Toasts*

74   *Fish, Meat & Poultry*

106   *Vegetarian*

126   *Index*

Introduction

irst impressions are impressions that last, and the dramatic impact that a beautifully presented, delicious and fragrant starter or first course can have on family and friends will not only make them hungry for more but will also leave them

with some unforgettable memories to savour forever. Starters can be as elegant or wholesome and as rich or refreshing as you desire – the only rule is to make sure that they are first courses that create a fantastic impression.

The variety of starters is almost endless. If it's a sophisticated dish suitable for an elegant dinner party that you are wanting, then you can choose from a refreshing soup, such as Chilled Prawn and Cucumber Soup, a delicate mousse, such as Sea Trout Mousse or something more unusual, such as Smoked Salmon and Rice Salad Parcels. Alternatively, for a more informal occasion you might want to make a classic Caesar Salad, a succulent Risotto with Four Cheeses or a tasty Herbed Pâté Pie.

Your choice of first course should take its cue from the food you intend to serve as a main course. Choose with care, as the

starter will set the tone for the rest of the meal. If you are serving a roast meat or heavy stew as the main course, select something fairly light, such as Prawn, Egg and Avocado Mousse, or Marinated Asparagus and Langoustine. If, on the other hand, you are barbecuing fish or grilling chicken you could decide on something more elaborate and filling, such as Creamy Courgette and Dolcelatte Soup or an elegant terrine, such as Haddock and Smoked Salmon Terrine.

Don't be afraid of mixing and matching starters and main courses from different cuisines – for example, a Malayan Prawn Laksa would go well with a French or Italian-style meal, and crunchy Deep-fried Whitebait could happily come before

a creamy curry or a Mexican dish – it's taste and texture that are the important factors to take into consideration.

There are over a hundred first courses in this book, so whether you want soups or salads, meat or fish, hot or cold dishes or classic or exotic recipes there's a first course here to match every main course and to impress any guest.

Soups

Whether a refreshing, chilled starter, such as Melon and Basil Soup, a French classic – Fish Soup with Rouille, for example – or something more unusual, such as Malayan Prawn Laksa, soups are one of the most simple and most popular ways of starting a gourmet meal.

Cold Cucumber and Yogurt Soup

This refreshing cold soup uses the classic combination of cucumber and yogurt, with the added flavour of garlic and pleasant crunch of walnuts.

INGREDIENTS

Serves 5–6

1 cucumber

4 garlic cloves

2.5ml/½ tsp salt

75g/3oz/¾ cup walnut pieces

40g/1½ oz day-old bread, torn into pieces

30ml/2 tbsp walnut or sunflower oil

400ml/14fl oz/1⅔ cups sheep's or
   cow's yogurt

120ml/4fl oz/½ cup cold water or chilled
   still mineral water

5–10ml/1–2 tsp lemon juice

40g/1½oz/scant ½ cup walnuts, chopped,
   to garnish

olive oil, for drizzling

dill sprigs, to garnish

1 Cut the cucumber into two and peel one half of it. Dice the cucumber flesh and set aside.

2 Using a large pestle and mortar, crush the garlic and salt together well, then add the walnuts and bread.

3 When the mixture is smooth, add the walnut or sunflower oil slowly and combine well.

4 Transfer the walnut and bread mixture to a large bowl then beat in the cow's or sheep's yogurt and the diced cucumber.

5 Add the cold water or mineral water and lemon juice to taste.

6 Pour the soup into chilled soup bowls to serve. Garnish with the chopped walnuts, a little olive oil drizzled over the nuts and sprigs of dill.

COOK'S TIP

If you prefer your soup smooth, purée it in a food processor or blender before serving.

Chilled Tomato and Sweet Pepper Soup

This recipe was inspired by the Spanish gazpacho, the difference being that this soup is cooked first, and then chilled.

INGREDIENTS

Serves 4

2 red peppers, halved, cored and seeded

45ml/3 tbsp olive oil

1 onion, finely chopped

2 garlic cloves, crushed

675g/1½ lb ripe well-flavoured tomatoes

150ml/¼ pint/⅔ cup red wine

600ml/1 pint/2½ cups chicken stock

salt and ground black pepper

snipped fresh chives, to garnish

For the croûtons

2 slices white bread, crusts removed

60ml/4 tbsp olive oil

1 Cut each red pepper half into quarters. Place skin side up on a grill rack and cook until the skins are charred. Transfer to a bowl and cover with a plate or pop into a polythene bag and seal.

2 Heat the oil in a large pan. Add the onion and garlic and cook gently until soft. Meanwhile, remove the skin from the peppers and roughly chop the flesh. Cut the tomatoes into chunks.

3 Add the peppers and tomatoes to the pan, then cover and cook gently for 10 minutes. Add the wine and cook for a further 5 minutes, then add the stock and salt and pepper and continue to simmer for 20 minutes.

4 To make the croûtons, cut the bread into cubes. Heat the oil in a small frying pan, add the bread and fry until golden. Drain on kitchen paper and store in an airtight box.

5 Process the soup in a blender or food processor until smooth. Pour into a clean glass or ceramic bowl and leave to cool thoroughly before chilling in the fridge for at least 3 hours. When the soup is cold, season to taste.

6 Serve the soup in bowls, topped with the croûtons and garnished with snipped chives.

Pear and Watercress Soup

The pears in the soup are complemented beautifully by Stilton croûtons. Their flavours make them natural partners.

INGREDIENTS

Serves 6

1 bunch watercress

4 pears, sliced

900ml/1½ pints/3¾ cups chicken stock, preferably home-made

120ml/4fl oz/½ cup double cream

juice of 1 lime

salt and ground black pepper

For the croûtons

25g/1oz/2 tbsp butter

15ml/1 tbsp olive oil

200g/7oz/3 cups cubed stale bread

150g/5oz/1 cup chopped Stilton

1 Keep back about a third of the watercress leaves. Place the rest of the leaves and stalks in a pan with the pears, stock and a little seasoning. Simmer for about 15–20 minutes. Reserving some watercress leaves for garnishing, add the rest of the leaves and then purée in a blender or food processor until smooth.

2 Put the mixture into a bowl and stir in the cream and the lime juice to mix the flavours thoroughly. Season again to taste. Pour all the soup back into a pan and reheat, stirring gently until warmed through.

3 To make the croûtons, melt the butter and oil and fry the bread cubes until golden brown. Drain on kitchen paper. Put the cheese on top and heat under a hot grill until bubbling. Reheat the soup and pour into bowls. Divide the croûtons and the reserved watercress leaves between the bowls and serve immediately.

Tortellini Chanterelle Broth

The savoury-sweet quality of chanterelle mushrooms combines well in a simple broth with spinach-and-ricotta-filled tortellini. The addition of a little sherry creates a lovely warming effect.

INGREDIENTS

Serves 4

350g/12oz fresh spinach and ricotta
    tortellini, or 175g/6oz dried
1.2 litres/2 pints/5 cups chicken stock
75ml/5 tbsp dry sherry
175g/6oz fresh chanterelle mushrooms,
    trimmed and sliced, or 15g/½ oz/½ cup
    dried chanterelles
chopped fresh parsley, to garnish

1 Cook the tortellini according to the packet instructions.

2 Bring the chicken stock to the boil, add the dry sherry and fresh or dried mushrooms and simmer for 10 minutes.

3 Strain the tortellini, add to the stock, then ladle the broth into four warmed soup bowls, making sure each contains the same proportions of tortellini and mushrooms. Garnish with the chopped parsley and serve.

Spanish Garlic Soup

This is a simple and satisfying soup, made with one of the most popular ingredients in the Mediterranean region – garlic!

INGREDIENTS

Serves 4

30ml/2 tbsp olive oil

4 large garlic cloves, peeled

4 slices French bread, 5mm/¼ in thick

15ml/1 tbsp paprika

1 litre/1¾ pints/4 cups beef stock

1.5ml/¼ tsp ground cumin

pinch of saffron strands

4 eggs

salt and ground black pepper

chopped fresh parsley, to garnish

1 Preheat the oven to 230°C/450°F/Gas 8. Heat the oil in a large pan. Add the whole garlic cloves and cook until golden. Remove and set aside. Fry the bread in the oil until golden, then set aside.

COOK'S TIP

Use home-made beef stock for the best flavour or buy prepared stock from your supermarket – you'll find it in the chilled counter. Never use stock cubes as they contain too much salt.

2 Add the paprika to the pan, and fry for a few seconds, stirring. Stir in the beef stock, the cumin and saffron, then add the reserved fried garlic, crushing the cloves with the back of a wooden spoon. Season with salt and ground black pepper then cook for about 5 minutes.

3 Ladle the soup into four ovenproof bowls and gently break an egg into each one. Place the slices of fried French bread on top of the eggs and place in the oven for about 3–4 minutes, or until the eggs are set. Sprinkle with chopped fresh parsley and serve at once.

French Onion and Morel Soup

French onion soup is appreciated for its light beefy taste. There are few improvements to be made to this classic soup, but a few richly scented morel mushrooms will impart a worthwhile flavour.

INGREDIENTS

Serves 4

50g/2oz/4 tbsp unsalted butter, plus extra
   for spreading

15ml/1 tbsp vegetable oil

3 onions, sliced

900ml/1½ pints/3¾ cups beef stock

75ml/5 tbsp Madeira or sherry

8 dried morel mushrooms

4 slices French bread

75g/3oz Gruyère, Beaufort or Fontina
   cheese, grated

30ml/2 tbsp chopped fresh parsley

1 Melt the butter with the oil in a large frying pan, then add the sliced onions and cook gently for 10–15 minutes until the onions are a rich mahogany brown colour.

2 Transfer the browned onions to a large saucepan, cover with beef stock, add the Madeira or sherry and the dried morels, then simmer for 20 minutes.

COOK'S TIP

The flavour and richness of this soup will improve with keeping. Chill for up to 5 days.

3 Preheat the grill to a moderate temperature and toast the French bread on both sides. Spread one side with butter and heap with the grated cheese. Ladle the soup into four flameproof bowls, float the cheesy toasts on top and grill until they are crisp and brown. Alternatively, grill the cheese-topped toast, then place one slice in each warmed soup bowl before ladling the hot soup over it. The toast will float to the surface. Scatter over the chopped fresh parsley and serve.

Wild Mushroom Soup

Wild mushrooms are expensive, but dried porcini have an intense flavour, so only a small quantity is needed. The beef stock may seem unusual in a vegetable soup, but it helps to strengthen the earthy flavour of the mushrooms.

INGREDIENTS

Serves 4

25g/1oz/1 cup dried porcini mushrooms

30ml/2 tbsp olive oil

15g/½ oz/1 tbsp butter

2 leeks, thinly sliced

2 shallots, roughly chopped

1 garlic clove, roughly chopped

225g/8oz/3 cups fresh wild mushrooms

about 1.2 litres/2 pints/5 cups beef stock

2.5ml/½ tsp dried thyme

150ml/¼ pint/⅔ cup double cream

salt and ground black pepper

thyme sprigs, to garnish

1 Put the dried porcini in a bowl, add 250ml/8fl oz/1 cup warm water and leave to soak for 20–30 minutes. Lift out of the liquid and squeeze over the bowl to remove as much of the soaking liquid as possible. Strain all the liquid and reserve to use later. Finely chop the porcini.

2 Heat the oil and butter in a large saucepan until foaming. Add the sliced leeks, chopped shallots and garlic and cook gently for about 5 minutes, stirring frequently, until soft.

3 Chop or slice the fresh wild mushrooms and add to the pan. Stir over a medium heat for a few minutes until they begin to soften. Pour in the stock and bring to the boil. Add the porcini, their soaking liquid, the dried thyme and salt and ground black pepper. Lower the heat, half cover the pan and simmer the soup gently for 30 minutes, stirring occasionally.

4 Pour about three-quarters of the soup into a blender or food processor and process until very smooth. Return the purée to the soup remaining in the pan, stir in the cream and heat through. Check the consistency and add a little more stock or water if the soup is too thick. Taste for seasoning. Serve hot garnished with thyme sprigs.

Fresh Tomato Soup

Intensely flavoured sun-ripened tomatoes need little embellishment in this fresh-tasting soup. If you buy from the supermarket, choose the juiciest looking ones and add the amount of sugar and vinegar necessary, depending on their natural sweetness. On a hot day this Italian soup is also delicious chilled.

INGREDIENTS

Serves 6

1.3–1.6kg/3–3½ lb ripe tomatoes

400ml/14fl oz/1⅔ cups chicken or
    vegetable stock

45ml/3 tbsp sun-dried tomato paste

30–45ml/2–3 tbsp balsamic vinegar

10–15ml/2–3 tsp caster sugar

small handful of basil leaves

salt and ground black pepper

basil leaves, to garnish

toasted cheese croûtes and crème fraîche,
    to serve

1 Plunge the tomatoes into boiling water for 30 seconds, then refresh in cold water. Peel away the skins and quarter the tomatoes. Put them in a large saucepan and pour over the chicken or vegetable stock. Bring just to the boil, reduce the heat, cover and simmer the mixture gently for 10 minutes until the tomatoes are pulpy.

2 Stir in the tomato paste, vinegar, sugar and basil. Season with salt and pepper, then cook gently, stirring, for 2 minutes. Process the soup in a blender or food processor, then return to the pan and reheat gently. Serve in bowls topped with one or two toasted cheese croûtes and a spoonful of crème fraîche, garnished with basil leaves.

Broccoli Soup with Garlic Toast

This is an Italian recipe, originating from Rome. For the best flavour and colour, use the freshest broccoli you can find.

INGREDIENTS

Serves 6

675g/1½ lb broccoli spears

1.75 litres/3 pints/7½ cups chicken or vegetable stock

salt and ground black pepper

30ml/2 tbsp fresh lemon juice

freshly grated Parmesan cheese (optional), to serve

For the garlic toast

6 slices white bread

1 large clove garlic, halved

1 Using a small sharp knife, peel the broccoli stems, starting from the base of the stalks and pulling gently up towards the florets. (The peel comes off very easily.) Chop the broccoli into small chunks.

2 Bring the stock to the boil in a large saucepan. Add the chopped broccoli and simmer for 30 minutes, or until soft.

COOK'S TIP

As this is an Italian recipe, choose a really good quality Parmesan cheese, if you are using it. The very best is Italy's own Parmigiano-Reggiano.

3 Purée about half of the soup in a blender or food processor and then mix into the rest of the soup. Season with salt, pepper and lemon juice.

4 Just before serving, reheat the soup to just below boiling point. Toast the bread, rub with garlic and cut into quarters. Place 3 or 4 pieces of toast in the base of each soup plate. Ladle on the soup. Serve at once, with grated Parmesan cheese if wished.

Melon and Basil Soup

This is a deliciously refreshing, chilled fruit soup, just right for a hot summer's day.

Serves 4–6

2 Charentais or rock melons

75 g/3 oz/scant ½ cup caster sugar

175 ml/6 fl oz/¾ cup water

finely grated rind and juice of 1 lime

45 ml/3 tbsp shredded fresh basil, plus
   whole leaves, to garnish

1 Cut the melons in half across the middle. Scrape out the seeds and discard. Using a melon baller, scoop out 20–24 balls and set aside for the garnish. Scoop out the remaining flesh and place in a blender or food processor.

2 Place the sugar, water and lime rind in a small pan over a low heat. Stir until dissolved, bring to the boil and simmer for 2–3 minutes. Remove from the heat and leave to cool slightly. Pour half the mixture into the blender or food processor with the melon flesh. Blend until smooth, adding the remaining syrup and lime juice to taste.

3 Pour the mixture into a bowl, stir in the shredded basil and chill. Serve garnished with whole basil leaves and the reserved melon balls.

COOK'S TIP

Add the syrup in two stages, as the amount of sugar needed will depend on the sweetness of the melon.

Chilled Almond Soup

Unless you are prepared to spend time pounding all the ingredients for this soup by hand, a food processor is essential. Then you'll find that this Spanish soup is simple to make and refreshing to eat on a hot day.

Serves 6

115 g/4 oz fresh white bread

750 ml/1¼ pints/3 cups cold water

115 g/4 oz/1 cup blanched almonds

2 garlic cloves, sliced

75 ml/5 tbsp olive oil

25 ml/1½ tbsp sherry vinegar

salt and freshly ground black pepper

For the garnish

toasted flaked almonds

seedless green and black grapes, halved
   and skinned

1 Break the bread into a bowl and pour 150 ml/¼ pint/⅔ cup of the water on top. Leave for 5 minutes.

2 Put the almonds and garlic in a blender or food processor and process until finely ground. Blend in the soaked bread.

3 Gradually add the oil until the mixture forms a smooth paste. Add the sherry vinegar, then the remaining cold water and process until smooth.

4 Transfer to a bowl and season with salt and pepper, adding a little more water if the soup is too thick. Chill for at least 2–3 hours. Serve scattered with the toasted almonds and grapes.

Spinach and Rice Soup

Use very fresh, young spinach leaves in the preparation of this light and fresh-tasting soup.

INGREDIENTS

Serves 4

675g/1½ lb fresh spinach, washed
45ml/3 tbsp extra virgin olive oil
1 small onion, finely chopped
2 garlic cloves, finely chopped
1 small fresh red chilli, seeded and
   finely chopped
115g/4oz/generous 1 cup risotto rice
1.2 litres/2 pints/5 cups vegetable stock
salt and ground black pepper
60ml/4 tbsp grated Pecorino cheese

1 Place the spinach in a large pan with just the water that clings to its leaves after washing. Add a large pinch of salt. Heat gently until the spinach has wilted, then remove from the heat and drain, reserving any liquid.

2 Either chop the spinach finely using a large knife or place in a food processor and process to a fairly coarse purée.

COOK'S TIP

Pecorino, made from sheep's milk, has a slightly sharper taste than its cow's milk counterpart, Parmesan. However, if you cannot find it, use Parmesan instead.

3 Heat the oil in a large saucepan and gently cook the onion, garlic and chilli for 4–5 minutes until softened. Stir in the rice until well coated, then pour in the stock and reserved spinach liquid. Bring to the boil, lower the heat and simmer for 10 minutes. Add the spinach, with salt and ground black pepper to taste. Cook for a further 5–7 minutes, until the rice is tender. Check the seasoning and adjust if needed. Serve with the Pecorino cheese.

Creamy Courgette and Dolcelatte Soup

The beauty of this soup is its delicate colour, its creamy texture and its subtle taste. If you prefer a more pronounced cheese flavour, use Gorgonzola instead of Dolcelatte.

INGREDIENTS

Serves 4–6

30 ml/2 tbsp olive oil

15 g/½ oz/1 tbsp butter

1 medium onion, roughly chopped

900 g/2 lb courgettes, trimmed and sliced

5 ml/1 tsp dried oregano

about 600 ml/1 pint/2½ cups vegetable
    stock

115 g/4 oz Dolcelatte cheese, rind
    removed, diced

300 ml/½ pint/1¼ cups single cream

salt and freshly ground black pepper

To garnish

sprigs of fresh oregano

extra Dolcelatte cheese

1 Heat the oil and butter in a large saucepan until foaming. Add the onion and cook gently for about 5 minutes, stirring frequently, until softened but not brown.

2 Add the courgettes and oregano, with salt and pepper to taste. Cook over a medium heat for 10 minutes, stirring frequently.

3 Pour in the stock and bring to the boil, stirring frequently. Lower the heat, half-cover the pan and simmer gently, stirring occasionally, for about 30 minutes. Stir in the diced Dolcelatte until it is melted.

4 Process the soup in a blender or food processor until smooth, then press through a sieve into a clean pan.

5 Add two-thirds of the cream and stir over a low heat until hot, but not boiling. Check the consistency and add more stock if the soup is too thick. Taste and adjust seasoning if necessary.

6 Pour into heated bowls. Swirl in the remaining cream, garnish with fresh oregano and extra Dolcelatte cheese, crumbled, and serve.

Hungarian Sour Cherry Soup

Particularly popular in summer, this fruit soup is typical of Hungarian cooking. The recipe makes good use of plump, sour cherries. Fruit soups are thickened with flour, and a touch of salt is added to help bring out the flavour of the cold soup.

INGREDIENTS

Serves 4

15 ml/1 tbsp plain flour

120 ml/4 fl oz/¹⁄₂ cup soured cream

a generous pinch of salt

5 ml/1 tsp caster sugar

225 g/8 oz/1¹⁄₂ cups fresh sour or morello
    cherries, stoned

900 ml/1¹⁄₂ pints/3³⁄₄ cups water

50 g/2 oz/¹⁄₄ cup granulated sugar

1 In a bowl, blend the flour with the soured cream until smooth, then add the salt and caster sugar.

2 Put the cherries in a pan with the water and granulated sugar. Gently poach for about 10 minutes.

3 Remove from the heat and set aside 30 ml/2 tbsp of the cooking liquid as a garnish. Stir another 30 ml/2 tbsp of the cherry liquid into the flour and soured cream mixture, then pour this on to the cherries.

4 Return to the heat. Bring to the boil, then simmer gently for 5–6 minutes.

5 Remove from the heat, cover with clear film and leave to cool. Add extra salt if necessary. Serve with the reserved cooking liquid swirled in.

Spinach and Tofu Soup

This is an extremely delicate and mild-flavoured soup, which can be used to counterbalance the heat from a hot Thai curry.

INGREDIENTS

Serves 4–6

30 ml/2 tbsp dried shrimps

1 litre/1¾ pints/4 cups chicken stock

225 g/8 oz fresh tofu, drained and cut into
  2 cm/¾ in cubes

30 ml/2 tbsp fish sauce

350 g/12 oz fresh spinach

freshly ground black pepper

2 spring onions, finely sliced, to garnish

1 Rinse and drain the dried shrimps. Combine the shrimps with the chicken stock in a large saucepan and bring to the boil. Add the tofu and simmer for about 5 minutes. Season with fish sauce and black pepper to taste.

2 Wash the spinach leaves thoroughly and tear into bite-size pieces. Add to the soup. Cook for another 1–2 minutes.

3 Pour the soup into warmed bowls, sprinkle the chopped spring onions on top to garnish, and serve.

Watercress and Orange Soup

This is a healthy and refreshing soup, which is just as good served either hot or chilled.

INGREDIENTS

Serves 4

1 large onion, chopped
15 ml/1 tbsp olive oil
2 bunches or bags of watercress
grated rind and juice of 1 large orange
600 ml/1 pint/2½ cups vegetable stock
150 ml/¼ pint/⅔ cup single cream
10 ml/2 tsp cornflour
salt and freshly ground black pepper
a little thick cream or natural yogurt,
    to garnish
4 orange wedges, to serve

1 Soften the onion in the oil in a large pan. Add the watercress, unchopped, to the onion. Cover and cook for about 5 minutes until the watercress is softened.

2 Add the orange rind and juice and the stock to the watercress mixture. Bring to the boil, cover and simmer for 10–15 minutes.

3 Blend or liquidize the soup thoroughly, and sieve if you want to increase the smoothness of the finished soup. Blend the cream with the cornflour until no lumps remain, then add to the soup. Season to taste.

4 Bring the soup gently back to the boil, stirring until just slightly thickened. Check the seasoning.

5 Serve the soup with a swirl of cream or yogurt, and a wedge of orange to squeeze in at the last moment.

6 If serving the soup chilled, thicken as above and leave to cool, before chilling in the refrigerator. Garnish with cream or yogurt and orange, as above.

Chilled Prawn and Cucumber Soup

If you've never served a chilled soup before, this is the one to try first. Delicious and light, it's the perfect way to celebrate summer.

Serves 4

25g/1oz/2 tbsp butter

2 shallots, finely chopped

2 garlic cloves, crushed

1 cucumber, peeled, seeded and diced

300ml/½ pint/1¼ cups milk

225g/8oz cooked peeled prawns

15ml/1 tbsp each finely chopped fresh
   mint, dill, chives and chervil

300ml/½ pint/1¼ cups whipping cream

salt and ground white pepper

For the garnish

30ml/2 tbsp crème fraîche or soured
   cream (optional)

4 large, cooked prawns, peeled with tail
   intact

fresh chives and dill

1 Melt the butter in a saucepan and cook the shallots and garlic over a low heat until soft but not coloured. Add the cucumber and cook the vegetables gently, stirring frequently, until tender.

2 Stir in the milk, bring almost to the boil, then lower the heat and simmer for 5 minutes. Tip the soup into a blender or food processor and purée until very smooth. Season to taste with salt and ground white pepper.

3 Pour the soup into a bowl and set aside to cool. When cool, stir in the prawns, chopped herbs and the whipping cream. Cover, transfer to the fridge and chill for at least 2 hours.

4 To serve, ladle the soup into four individual bowls and top each portion with a dollop of crème fraîche or soured cream, if using. Place a prawn over the edge of each dish. Garnish with the chives and dill.

COOK'S TIP

For a change try fresh or canned crabmeat, or cooked, flaked salmon fillet.

Gazpacho with Avocado Salsa

Tomatoes, cucumber and peppers form the basis of this classic, chilled soup. Add a spoonful of chunky, fresh avocado salsa and a scattering of croûtons for a delicious summer starter. This is quite a substantial soup, so follow with a light main course, such as grilled fish or chicken.

INGREDIENTS

Serves 4–6

2 slices day-old bread
600ml/1 pint/2½ cups chilled water
1kg/2¼ lb tomatoes
1 cucumber
1 red pepper, seeded and chopped
1 green chilli, seeded and chopped
2 garlic cloves, chopped
30ml/2 tbsp extra virgin olive oil
juice of 1 lime and 1 lemon
few drops of Tabasco sauce
salt and ground black pepper
handful of fresh basil, to garnish
8–12 ice cubes, to serve

For the croûtons
2–3 slices day-old bread, crusts removed
1 garlic clove, halved
15–30ml/1–2 tbsp olive oil

For the avocado salsa
1 ripe avocado
5ml/1 tsp lemon juice
2.5cm/1in piece cucumber, diced
½ red chilli, finely chopped

1 Make the soup first. In a shallow bowl, soak the day-old bread in 150ml/¼ pint/⅔ cup water for 5 minutes.

2 Meanwhile, place the tomatoes in a heatproof bowl; cover with boiling water. Leave for 30 seconds, then peel, seed and chop the flesh.

3 Thinly peel the cucumber, cut in half lengthways and scoop out the seeds with a teaspoon. Discard the seeds and chop the flesh.

4 Place the bread, tomatoes, cucumber, red pepper, chilli, garlic, oil, citrus juices, Tabasco and 450ml/¾ pint/scant 2 cups chilled water in a food processor or blender. Blend until mixed but still chunky. Season and chill well.

5 To make the croûtons, rub the slices of bread with the cut surface of the garlic clove. Cut the bread into cubes and place in a polythene bag with the olive oil. Seal the bag and shake until the bread cubes are coated with the oil. Heat a large non-stick frying pan and fry the croûtons over a medium heat until crisp and golden.

6 Just before serving make the avocado salsa. Halve the avocado, remove the stone, then peel and dice the flesh. Toss the avocado in the lemon juice to prevent it browning, then mix with the cucumber and chilli.

7 Ladle the soup into bowls, add the ice cubes, and top with a spoonful of avocado salsa. Garnish with the basil and hand round the croûtons separately.

COOK'S TIP
For a superior flavour choose Haas avocados with the rough-textured, almost black skins.

Hot-and-sour Soup

This light and invigorating soup originates from Thailand. It is traditionally served at the beginning of a formal Thai meal to stimulate the appetite.

INGREDIENTS

Serves 4

2 carrots

900ml/1½ pints/3¾ cups vegetable stock

2 Thai chillies, seeded and finely sliced

2 lemon grass stalks, outer leaves removed and each stalk cut into 3 pieces

4 kaffir lime leaves

2 garlic cloves, finely chopped

4 spring onions, finely sliced

5ml/1 tsp sugar

juice of 1 lime

45ml/3 tbsp chopped fresh coriander

salt, to taste

130g/4½ oz/1 cup Japanese tofu, sliced

1 To make carrot flowers, cut each carrot in half crossways, then, using a sharp knife, cut four V-shaped channels lengthways. Slice the carrots into thin rounds and set aside.

COOK'S TIP

Kaffir lime leaves have a distinctive citrus flavour. The fresh leaves can be bought from Asian shops, and some supermarkets now sell them dried.

2 Pour the vegetable stock into a large saucepan. Reserve 2.5ml/½ tsp of the chillies and add the rest to the pan with the lemon grass, lime leaves, garlic and half the spring onions. Bring to the boil, then reduce the heat and simmer for 20 minutes. Strain the stock and discard the flavourings.

3 Return the stock to the pan, add the reserved chillies and spring onions, the sugar, lime juice, coriander and salt to taste.

4 Simmer for 5 minutes, then add the carrot flowers and tofu slices, and cook the soup for a further 2 minutes until the carrot is just tender. Serve hot.

Malayan Prawn Laksa

This spicy prawn and noodle soup tastes just as good when made with fresh crab meat or any flaked cooked fish. If you are short of time or can't find all the spicy paste ingredients, buy ready-made laksa paste, which is available from Oriental stores.

INGREDIENTS

Serves 4

115g/4oz rice vermicelli or stir-fry
   rice noodles
15ml/1 tbsp vegetable or groundnut oil
600ml/1 pint/2½ cups fish stock
400ml/14fl oz/1⅔ cups thin coconut milk
30ml/2 tbsp *nam pla* (Thai fish sauce)
½ lime
16–24 cooked peeled prawns
salt and cayenne pepper
60ml/4 tbsp fresh coriander sprigs and
   leaves, chopped, to garnish

For the spicy paste
2 lemon grass stalks, finely chopped
2 fresh red chillies, seeded and chopped
2.5cm/1in piece fresh root ginger, peeled
   and sliced
2.5ml/½ tsp *blachan* (dried shrimp paste)
2 garlic cloves, chopped
2.5ml/½ tsp ground turmeric
30ml/2 tbsp tamarind paste

1 Cook the rice vermicelli or noodles in a large saucepan of boiling salted water according to the instructions on the packet. Tip into a large sieve or colander, then rinse under cold water and drain. Set aside and keep warm.

2 To make the spicy paste, place all the ingredients in a mortar and pound with a pestle. Or, if you prefer, put the ingredients in a food processor or blender and then process until a smooth paste is formed.

3 Heat the oil in a large saucepan, add the spicy paste and fry, stirring constantly, for a few moments to release all the flavours, but be careful not to let it burn.

4 Add the fish stock and coconut milk and bring to the boil. Stir in the *nam pla*, then simmer for 5 minutes. Season with salt and cayenne to taste, adding a squeeze of lime. Add the prawns and heat through for a few seconds.

5 Divide the noodles among three or four soup plates. Pour the soup over, making sure that each portion includes an equal number of prawns. Garnish with coriander and serve piping hot.

Prawn and Egg-knot Soup

An unusual and special soup, just right for a festive occasion.

INGREDIENTS

Serves 4

900 ml/1½ pints/3¾ cups kombu and
    bonito stock or instant dashi
5 ml/1 tsp soy sauce
a dash of sake or dry white wine
salt
1 spring onion, finely sliced, to garnish

For the prawn shinjo balls
200 g/7 oz raw large prawns, shelled,
    thawed if frozen
65 g/2½ oz cod fillet, skinned
5 ml/1 tsp egg white
5 ml/1 tsp sake or dry white wine
22.5 ml/4½ tsp cornflour or potato starch
2–3 drops of soy sauce

For the omelette
1 egg, beaten
a dash of mirin
oil, for frying

1 Devein the prawns. Process the prawns, cod, egg white, 5 ml/1 tsp sake or wine, cornflour or potato starch, soy sauce and a pinch of salt in a food processor or blender to make a sticky paste. Alternatively, finely chop the prawns and cod, crush them with the knife's blade and then pound them well in a mortar with a pestle, before adding the remaining ingredients.

2 Shape the mixture into four balls and steam them for 10 minutes over a high heat. Meanwhile, soak the spring onion for the garnish in cold water for 5 minutes, then drain.

3 To make the omelette, mix the egg with a pinch of salt and the mirin. Heat a little oil in a frying pan and pour in the egg, tilting the pan to coat it evenly. When the egg has set, turn the omelette over and cook for 30 seconds. Leave to cool.

4 Cut the omelette into long strips about 2 cm/¾ in wide. Knot each strip once, place in a sieve and rinse with hot water to remove excess oil. Bring the stock or dashi to the boil and add the soy sauce, a pinch of salt and a dash of sake or wine. Divide the prawn balls and the egg knots among four bowls. Pour in the soup, sprinkle with the spring onion and serve.

Hot and Sour Prawn Soup with Lemon Grass

This classic seafood soup, known as Tom Yam Goong, is probably the most popular and best-known soup from Thailand.

Serves 4–6

450 g/1 lb king prawns

1 litre/1¾ pints/4 cups chicken stock
 or water

3 lemon grass stalks

10 kaffir lime leaves, torn in half

225 g/8 oz can straw mushrooms, drained

45 ml/3 tbsp fish sauce

50 ml/2 fl oz/¼ cup lime juice

30 ml/2 tbsp chopped spring onion

15 ml/1 tbsp fresh coriander leaves

4 fresh red chillies, seeded and chopped

2 spring onions, finely chopped,
 to garnish

1 Shell and devein the prawns and set aside. Rinse the prawn shells and place in a large saucepan with the stock or water and bring to the boil.

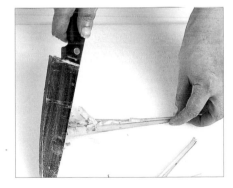

2 Bruise the lemon grass stalks with the blunt edge of a chopping knife and add them to the stock, together with half the lime leaves. Simmer gently for 5–6 minutes until the stalks change colour and the stock is fragrant.

3 Strain the stock, return to the saucepan and reheat. Add the mushrooms and prawns, then cook until the prawns turn pink.

4 Stir in the fish sauce, lime juice, spring onion, coriander, red chillies and the rest of the lime leaves. Taste and adjust the seasoning. The soup should be sour, salty, spicy and hot. Garnish with finely chopped spring onions before serving.

Clam and Basil Soup

Subtly sweet and spicy, this soup is an ideal starter for serving as part of a celebration dinner.

INGREDIENTS

Serves 4–6

30 ml/2 tbsp olive oil

1 medium onion, finely chopped

leaves from 1 fresh or dried sprig of thyme, chopped or crumbled

2 garlic cloves, crushed

5–6 fresh basil leaves, plus extra to garnish

1.5–2.5 ml/¼–½ tsp crushed red chillies, to taste

1 litre/1¾ pints/4 cups fish stock

350 ml/12 fl oz/1½ cups passata

5 ml/1 tsp granulated sugar

90 g/3½ oz/scant 1 cup frozen peas

65 g/2½ oz/⅔ cup small pasta shapes, such as chifferini

225 g/8 oz frozen shelled clams

salt and freshly ground black pepper

1 Heat the oil in a large saucepan, add the onion and cook gently for about 5 minutes until softened but not coloured. Add the thyme, then stir in the garlic, basil leaves and chillies.

2 Add the stock, passata and sugar to the saucepan, with salt and pepper to taste. Bring to the boil, then lower the heat and simmer gently for 15 minutes, stirring from time to time. Add the frozen peas and cook for a further 5 minutes.

3 Add the pasta to the stock mixture and bring to the boil, stirring. Lower the heat and simmer for about 5 minutes or according to the packet instructions, stirring frequently, until the pasta is *al dente*.

4 Turn the heat down to low, add the frozen clams and heat through for 2–3 minutes. Taste and adjust the seasoning. Serve hot in warmed bowls, garnished with basil leaves.

COOK'S TIP

Frozen shelled clams are available at good fishmongers and supermarkets. If you can't get them, use bottled or canned clams in natural juice (not vinegar). Italian delicatessens sell jars of clams in their shells. These both look and taste delicious and are not too expensive. For a special occasion, stir some into the soup.

Fish Soup with Rouille

Making this soup is simplicity itself, yet the flavour suggests it is the product of painstaking preparation and complicated cooking.

INGREDIENTS

Serves 6

1kg/2¼ lb mixed fish
30ml/2 tbsp olive oil
1 onion, chopped
1 carrot, chopped
1 leek, chopped
2 large ripe tomatoes, chopped
1 red pepper, seeded and chopped
2 garlic cloves, peeled
150g/5oz/⅔ cup tomato purée
1 large fresh bouquet garni, containing 3
  parsley sprigs, 3 small celery sticks and
  3 bay leaves
300ml/½ pint/1¼ cups dry white wine
salt and ground black pepper

For the rouille

2 garlic cloves, roughly chopped
5ml/1 tsp coarse salt
1 thick slice of white bread, crust
  removed, soaked in water and then
  squeezed dry
1 fresh red chilli, seeded and roughly
  chopped
45ml/3 tbsp olive oil
salt, to taste
pinch of cayenne pepper (optional)

For the garnish

12 slices of baguette, toasted in the oven
50g/2oz Gruyère cheese, finely grated

COOK'S TIP

Any firm fish can be used for this recipe. If you use whole fish, include the heads, which enhance the flavour of the soup.

1 Cut the fish into 7.5cm/3in chunks, removing any obvious bones. Heat the olive oil in a large saucepan, then add the prepared fish and chopped vegetables. Stir gently until the vegetables begin to colour.

2 Now add all the other soup ingredients, then pour in just enough cold water to cover the mixture. Season well and bring to just below boiling point, then lower the heat so that the soup is barely simmering, cover and cook for 1 hour.

3 Meanwhile, make the rouille. Put the garlic and coarse salt in a mortar and crush to a paste with a pestle. Add the soaked bread and chilli and pound until smooth, or purée in a food processor. Whisk in the olive oil, a drop at a time, to make a smooth, shiny sauce that resembles mayonnaise. Season with salt and add a pinch of cayenne if you like. Set aside.

4 Lift out and discard the bouquet garni. Purée the soup in batches in a food processor, then strain through a fine sieve into a clean pan, pushing the solids through with a ladle.

5 Reheat the soup but do not boil. Check the seasoning and ladle into individual bowls. Top each with two slices of toasted baguette, a spoonful of rouille and some grated Gruyère.

Consommé with Agnolotti

Prawns, crab and chicken jostle for the upper hand in this rich and satisfying consommé.

Serves 4–6

75 g/3 oz cooked peeled prawns

75 g/3 oz canned crab meat, drained

5 ml/1 tsp finely grated fresh root ginger

15 ml/l tbsp fresh white breadcrumbs

5 ml/l tsp light soy sauce

1 spring onion, finely chopped

1 garlic clove, crushed

1 egg white, beaten

400 g/14 oz can chicken or fish consommé

30 ml/2 tbsp sherry or vermouth

salt and freshly ground black pepper

For the pasta

200 g/7 oz/1¾ cups plain flour

pinch of salt

2 eggs

10 ml/2 tsp cold water

For the garnish

50 g/2 oz cooked peeled prawns

fresh coriander leaves

1 To make the pasta, sift the flour and salt on to a clean work surface and make a well in the centre with your hand.

2 Put the eggs and water into the well. Using a fork, beat the eggs gently together, then gradually draw in the flour from the sides, to make a thick paste.

3 When the mixture becomes too stiff to use a fork, use your hands to mix to a firm dough. Knead the dough for about 5 minutes until smooth. Wrap in clear film to prevent it drying out and leave to rest for 20-30 minutes.

4 Meanwhile, put the prawns, crab meat, ginger, breadcrumbs, soy sauce, spring onion, garlic and seasoning into a food processor or blender and process until smooth.

5 Once the pasta has rested, roll it into thin sheets. Stamp out 32 rounds 5 cm/2 in in diameter, using a fluted pastry cutter.

6 Place 5 ml/1 tsp of the filling in the centre of half the pasta rounds. Brush the edges of each round with egg white and sandwich with a second round on top. Pinch the edges together to stop the filling seeping out.

7 Cook the pasta in a large pan of boiling, salted water for 5 minutes (cook in batches to stop them sticking together). Remove and drop into a bowl of cold water for 5 seconds before placing on a tray. (You can make these pasta shapes a day in advance. Cover with clear film and store in the fridge.)

8 Heat the consommé in a pan with the sherry or vermouth. Add the cooked pasta shapes and simmer for 1–2 minutes.

9 Serve the pasta in soup bowls covered with hot consommé. Garnish with peeled prawns and coriander leaves.

Pâtés, Terrines & Soufflés

Pâtés have a wholesome, comforting appeal and are as simple and delicious as they look, whereas the complexity of a glamorous, layered terrine or delicate soufflé is deceptive. Whether you are catering for a family gathering or a formal dinner there are recipes here for every occasion.

Smoked Salmon Pâté

Making this pâté in individual ramekins wrapped in extra smoked salmon gives a really special presentation. Taste the mousse as you are making it as some people prefer more lemon juice and salt and pepper.

INGREDIENTS

Serves 4

350g/12oz thinly sliced smoked salmon
  (wild if possible)
150ml/¼ pint/⅔ cup double cream
finely grated rind and juice of 1 lemon
salt and ground black pepper
melba toast, to serve

1 Line four small ramekin dishes with clear film. Then line the dishes with 115g/4oz of the smoked salmon cut into strips long enough to flop over the edges.

2 In a food processor fitted with a metal blade, process the rest of the salmon with the double cream, lemon rind and juice, salt and plenty of pepper.

3 Pack the lined ramekins with the smoked salmon pâté and wrap over the loose strips of salmon. Cover with clear film and chill for 30 minutes. Invert on to plates; serve with melba toast.

Smoked Haddock Pâté

Arbroath smokies are small haddock that are beheaded and gutted but not split before being salted and hot-smoked, creating a great flavour.

INGREDIENTS

Serves 6

3 large Arbroath smokies, about
   225g/8oz each
275g/10oz/1¼ cups medium-fat
   soft cheese
3 eggs, beaten
30–45ml/2–3 tbsp lemon juice
ground black pepper
chervil sprigs, to garnish
lemon wedges and lettuce leaves, to serve

1 Preheat the oven to 160°C/
325°F/Gas 3. Butter six
ramekin dishes.

2 Lay the smokies in a baking
dish and heat through in the
oven for 10 minutes. Carefully
remove the skin and bones from
the smokies, then flake the flesh
into a bowl.

3 Mash the fish with a fork and
work in the cheese, then the
eggs. Add lemon juice and pepper.

4 Divide the fish mixture among
the ramekins and place in a
roasting tin. Pour hot water into
the roasting tin to come halfway
up the dishes. Bake for 30 minutes,
until just set.

5 Allow to cool for 2–3 minutes,
then run a knife point around
the edge of each dish and invert on
to a warmed plate. Garnish with
chervil sprigs and serve with the
lemon wedges and lettuce.

Chicken Liver Pâté

This rich-tasting, smooth pâté will keep in the fridge for about 3 days. Serve with thick slices of hot toast or warmed bread – a rustic olive oil bread such as ciabatta would be a good partner.

INGREDIENTS

Serves 8

115g/4oz chicken livers, thawed if frozen, trimmed

1 small garlic clove, chopped

15ml/1 tbsp sherry

30ml/2 tbsp brandy

50g/2oz/¼ cup butter, melted

2.5ml/¼ tsp salt

fresh herbs and black peppercorns, to garnish

hot toast or warmed bread, to serve

1 Preheat the oven to 150°C/ 300°F/Gas 2. Place the chicken livers and chopped garlic in a food processor or blender and process until they are smooth.

2 With the motor running, gradually add the sherry, brandy, melted butter and salt.

3 Pour the liver mixture into two 7.5cm/3in ramekins. Cover the tops with foil but do not allow the foil to come down the sides too far.

4 Place the ramekins in a small roasting pan and pour in boiling water so that it comes about halfway up the sides of the ramekins.

5 Carefully transfer the pan to the oven and bake the pâté for 20 minutes. Leave to cool to room temperature, then remove the ramekins from the pan and chill until needed. Serve the pâté with toast or bread, garnished with herbs and peppercorns.

Herbed Pâté Pie

Serve this highly flavoured pâté with a glass of Pilsner beer for a change from wine.

Serves 10

675g/1½ lb minced pork
350g/12oz pork liver
350g/12oz/2 cups diced cooked ham
1 small onion, finely chopped
30ml/2 tbsp chopped fresh parsley
5ml/1 tsp German mustard
30ml/2 tbsp Kirsch
5ml/1 tsp salt
beaten egg, for sealing and glazing
25g/1oz sachet aspic jelly
250ml/8fl oz/1 cup boiling water
ground black pepper
mustard, bread and dill pickles, to serve

For the pastry

450g/1lb/4 cups plain flour
pinch of salt
275g/10oz/1¼ cups butter
2 eggs plus 1 egg yolk
30ml/2 tbsp water

1 Preheat the oven to 200°C/400°F/Gas 6. To make the pastry, sift the flour and salt and rub in the butter. Beat the eggs, egg yolk and water, add to the dry ingredients and mix.

2 Knead the dough briefly until smooth. Roll out two-thirds on a lightly floured surface and use to line a 10 x 25cm/4 x 10in hinged loaf tin. Trim any excess dough.

3 Process half the pork and all of the liver until fairly smooth. Stir in the remaining minced pork, ham, onion, parsley, mustard, Kirsch, salt and black pepper to taste.

4 Spoon the filling into the tin, smoothing it down and then levelling the surface.

5 Roll out the remaining pastry on the lightly floured surface and use it to top the pie, sealing the edges with some of the beaten egg. Decorate with the pastry trimmings and glaze with the remaining beaten egg. Using a fork, make 3 or 4 holes in the top, for the steam to escape.

6 Bake for 40 minutes, then reduce the oven temperature to 180°C/350°F/Gas 4 and cook for a further hour. Cover the pastry with foil if the top begins to brown too much. Allow the pie to cool in the tin.

7 Make up the aspic jelly, using the boiling water. Stir to dissolve, then allow to cool.

8 Make a small hole near the edge of the pie with a skewer, then pour in the aspic through a greaseproof paper funnel. Chill for at least 2 hours before serving the pie in slices with mustard, bread and dill pickles.

Prawn, Egg and Avocado Mousse

A light and creamy mousse with lots of chunky texture and a great mix of flavours. Serve on the same day you make it but chill really well first.

INGREDIENTS

Serves 6

a little olive oil

1 sachet gelatine

juice and rind of 1 lemon

60ml/4 tbsp good-quality mayonnaise

60ml/4 tbsp chopped fresh dill

5ml/1 tsp anchovy essence

5ml/1 tsp Worcestershire sauce

1 large avocado, ripe but just firm

4 hard-boiled eggs, peeled and chopped

175g/6oz/1 cup cooked prawns (roughly chopped if large)

250ml/8fl oz/1 cup double or whipping cream, lightly whipped

2 egg whites, whisked

salt and ground black pepper

dill or parsley sprigs, to garnish

warmed granary bread or toast, to serve

1 Prepare six small ramekins. Lightly grease the dishes with olive oil, then wrap a greaseproof paper collar around the top of each and secure with tape. This ensures that you can fill the dishes as high as you like, and the extra mixture will be supported while setting and it will look really dramatic when you remove the paper. Alternatively, prepare just one small soufflé dish.

2 Dissolve the gelatine in the lemon juice with 15ml/1 tbsp hot water in a small bowl set over hot water, until clear, stirring occasionally. Allow to cool slightly then blend in the lemon rind, mayonnaise, dill and and anchovy essence and Worcestershire sauce.

3 In a medium bowl mash the avocado; add the eggs and prawns. Stir in the gelatine mixture and then fold in the cream, egg whites and seasoning to taste. When evenly blended spoon into the ramekins or soufflé dish and chill for 3–4 hours. Garnish with the herbs and serve with bread or toast.

COOK'S TIP

Other fish can make a good alternative to prawns. Try substituting the same quantity of smoked trout or salmon, or cooked crab meat.

Sea Trout Mousse

This deliciously creamy mousse makes a little sea trout go a long way. It is equally good made with salmon if sea trout is unavailable. Serve with crisp melba toast or triangles of lightly toasted pitta bread.

Serves 6

250g/9oz sea trout fillet

120ml/4fl oz/½ cup fish stock

2 gelatine leaves, or 15ml/1 tbsp powdered gelatine

juice of ½ lemon

30ml/2 tbsp dry sherry or dry vermouth

30ml/2 tbsp freshly grated Parmesan

300ml/½ pint/1¼ cups whipping cream

2 egg whites

15ml/1 tbsp sunflower oil, for greasing

salt and ground white pepper

For the garnish

5cm/2in piece cucumber, with peel, thinly sliced and halved

fresh dill or chervil

1 Put the sea trout in a shallow pan. Pour in the fish stock and heat to simmering point. Poach the fish for about 3–4 minutes, until it is lightly cooked. Strain the stock into a jug and leave the trout to cool slightly.

2 Add the gelatine to the hot stock and stir until it has dissolved completely. Set aside until required.

3 When the trout is cool enough to handle, remove the skin and flake the flesh. Pour the stock into a food processor or blender. Process briefly, then gradually add the flaked trout, lemon juice, sherry or vermouth and Parmesan through the feeder tube, continuing to process the mixture until it is smooth. Scrape into a large bowl and leave to cool completely.

4 Lightly whip the cream in a bowl; fold it into the cold trout mixture. Season to taste, then cover with clear film and chill in the fridge until the mousse is just starting to set. It should have the consistency of mayonnaise.

5 In a grease-free bowl, beat the egg whites with a pinch of salt until they are softly peaking. Then using a large metal spoon, stir about one-third of the egg whites into the sea trout mixture to slacken it slightly, then fold in the rest.

6 Lightly grease six ramekins or similar individual serving dishes. Divide the mousse among the prepared dishes and level the surface. Place in the fridge for 2–3 hours, until set. Just before serving, arrange a few slices of cucumber and a small herb sprig on top of each mousse and scatter over a little chopped dill or chervil too.

Salmon Rillettes

This is an economical way of serving salmon, with only a little fillet required per head.

INGREDIENTS

Serves 6

350g/12oz salmon fillets

175g/6oz/¾ cup butter, softened

1 celery stick, finely chopped

1 leek, white part only, finely chopped

1 bay leaf

150ml/¼ pint/⅔ cup dry white wine

115g/4oz smoked salmon trimmings

generous pinch of ground mace

60ml/4 tbsp fromage frais

salt and ground black pepper

salad leaves, to serve

1 Lightly season the salmon. Melt 25g/1oz/2 tbsp of the butter in a medium sauté pan. Add the celery and leek and cook for about 5 minutes. Add the salmon and bay leaf and pour the white wine over. Cover and cook for about 15 minutes until tender.

2 Strain the cooking liquid into a pan and boil until reduced to 30ml/2 tbsp. Cool. Meanwhile, melt 50g/2oz/4 tbsp of the remaining butter and gently cook the smoked salmon trimmings until it turns pale pink. Leave to cool.

3 Remove the skin and any bones from the salmon fillets. Flake the flesh into a bowl and add the reduced, cooled cooking liquid.

4 Beat in the remaining butter, with the ground mace and the fromage frais. Break up the cooked smoked salmon trimmings and fold into the salmon mixture with all the juices from the pan. Taste and adjust the seasoning if you need to.

5 Spoon the salmon mixture into a dish or terrine and smooth the top level. Cover with clear film and chill. The prepared mixture can be left in the fridge for up to 2 days.

6 To serve the salmon rillettes, shape the mixture into oval quenelles using two dessert spoons and arrange on individual plates with the salad leaves. Accompany the rillettes with brown bread or oatcakes, if you like.

Brandade of Salt Cod

There are almost as many versions of this creamy salt cod purée as there are regions of France. Some contain mashed potatoes, others truffles. This comparatively light recipe includes garlic, but you can omit it and serve the brandade on toasted slices of French bread rubbed with garlic if you prefer.

INGREDIENTS

Serves 6

200g/7oz salt cod
250ml/8fl oz/1 cup extra virgin olive oil
4 garlic cloves, crushed
250ml/8fl oz/1 cup whipping or
   double cream
ground white pepper
shredded spring onions, to garnish
herbed crispbread, to serve

1 Soak the fish in cold water for 24 hours, changing the water often. Drain. Cut into pieces, place in a shallow pan and pour in cold water to cover. Heat the water until simmering, then poach the fish for 8 minutes, until it is just cooked. Drain, then remove the skin and bone the cod carefully.

2 Combine the olive oil and garlic in a small saucepan and heat to just below boiling point. In another saucepan, heat the cream until it starts to simmer.

3 Put the cod into a food processor, process it briefly, then gradually add alternate amounts of the garlic-flavoured olive oil and cream, while keeping the machine running.

4 Once the mixture has the consistency of mashed potatoes add white pepper to taste, then scoop the branade into a serving bowl. Garnish with shredded spring onions and serve warm with herbed crispbread.

COOK'S TIP

You can purée the fish mixture in a mortar with a pestle. This gives a better texture, but is notoriously hard work.

Potted Salmon with Lemon and Dill

This sophisticated starter would be ideal for a dinner party. Preparation is done well in advance, so you can concentrate on the main course, or if you are really well organized, you can enjoy a pre-dinner conversation with your guests. If you cannot find fresh dill use 5ml/1 tsp dried dill instead.

INGREDIENTS

Serves 6

350g/12oz cooked salmon, skinned
150g/5oz/²⁄₃ cup butter, softened
rind and juice of 1 large lemon
10ml/2 tsp chopped fresh dill
salt and ground white pepper
75g/3oz/¾ cup flaked almonds,
   roughly chopped

1 Flake the salmon into a bowl and then place in a food processor together with two-thirds of the butter, the lemon rind and juice, half the dill, and plenty of salt and pepper. Blend until the mixture is quite smooth.

2 Mix in the flaked almonds. Check the seasoning and pack the mixture into small ramekins.

3 Scatter the other half of the dill over the top of each ramekin. Clarify the remaining butter, and pour over each ramekin to make a seal. Chill. Serve with crudités.

Potted Prawns

The tiny brown prawns that were traditionally used for potting are very fiddly to peel. Since they are rare nowadays, it is easier to use peeled cooked prawns instead.

INGREDIENTS

Serves 4

225g/8oz/2 cups shelled prawns

225g/8oz/1 cup butter

pinch of ground mace

salt, to taste

cayenne pepper

dill sprigs, to garnish

lemon wedges and thin slices of brown
   bread and butter, to serve

1 Chop a quarter of the prawns. Melt 115g/4oz/½ cup of the butter slowly, carefully skimming off any foam that rises to the surface with a metal spoon.

2 Stir all the prawns, the mace, salt and cayenne into the pan and heat gently without boiling. Pour the prawns and butter mixture into four individual pots and leave to cool.

3 Heat the remaining butter in a clean small saucepan, then carefully spoon the clear butter over the prawns, leaving behind the sediment.

4 Leave until the butter is almost set, then place a dill sprig in the centre of each pot. Leave to set completely, then cover and chill.

5 Transfer the prawns to room temperature 30 minutes before serving with lemon wedges for squeezing over and thin slices of brown bread and butter.

COOK'S TIP

If you prefer add a pinch of freshly grated nutmeg in place of the ground mace. The flavour is similar but it will not colour the dish.

Grilled Vegetable Terrine

A colourful, layered terrine, this starter uses all the vegetables that are associated with the Mediterranean and long, balmy summer evenings.

Serves 6

2 large red peppers, quartered, cored and seeded
2 large yellow peppers, quartered, cored and seeded
1 large aubergine, sliced lengthways
2 large courgettes, sliced lengthways
90ml/6 tbsp olive oil
1 large red onion, thinly sliced
75g/3oz/½ cup raisins
15ml/1 tbsp tomato purée
15ml/1 tbsp red wine vinegar
400ml/14fl oz/1⅔ cups tomato juice
15g/½oz/2 tbsp powdered gelatine
fresh basil leaves, to garnish

For the dressing

90ml/6 tbsp extra virgin olive oil
30ml/2 tbsp red wine vinegar
salt and ground black pepper

1 Place the prepared peppers skin side up under a hot grill and cook until the skins are blackened. Transfer to a bowl and cover with a plate. Leave to cool.

2 Arrange the aubergine and courgette slices on separate baking sheets. Brush them with a little oil and cook under the grill, turning occasionally, until they are tender and golden.

3 Heat the remaining olive oil in a frying pan, and add the sliced onion, raisins, tomato purée and red wine vinegar. Cook gently until the mixture is soft and syrupy. Set aside and leave to cool in the frying pan.

4 Line a 1.75 litre/3 pint/7½ cup terrine with clear film, (it helps if you lightly oil the terrine first) leaving a little hanging over the sides of the container.

5 Pour half the tomato juice into a saucepan, and sprinkle with the gelatine. Dissolve gently over a low heat, stirring to prevent any lumps from forming.

6 Place a layer of red peppers in the base of the terrine, and pour in enough of the tomato juice with gelatine to cover.

7 Continue layering the vegetables, pouring tomato juice over each layer. Finishing with a layer of red peppers. Add the remaining tomato juice to the pan, and pour into the terrine. Give it a sharp tap, to disperse the juice. Cover and chill until set.

8 To make the dressing, whisk together the oil and vinegar, and season. Turn out the terrine and remove the clear film. Serve in thick slices, drizzled with dressing and garnished with basil leaves.

COOK'S TIP

Ring the changes and use orange and green peppers along with or in place of the red and yellow ones. French beans, simply boiled first, would make a nice addition, as would a layer of peas or sweetcorn.

Roast Pepper Terrine

This terrine is perfect for a dinner party because it tastes better if made ahead. Prepare the salsa on the day of serving. Serve with a warmed Italian bread such as ciabatta or the flavoursome focaccia.

INGREDIENTS

Serves 8

8 peppers (red, yellow and orange)

675g/1½ lb/3 cups mascarpone cheese

3 eggs, separated

30ml/2 tbsp each roughly chopped flat leaf parsley and shredded basil

2 large garlic cloves, roughly chopped

2 red, yellow or orange peppers, seeded and roughly chopped

30ml/2 tbsp extra virgin olive oil

10ml/2 tsp balsamic vinegar

a few basil sprigs

salt and ground black pepper

1 Place the whole peppers under a hot grill for 8–10 minutes, turning frequently. Then put into a polythene bag until cold before skinning and seeding them. Chop seven of the peppers lengthways into thin strips.

2 Put the mascarpone cheese in a bowl with the egg yolks, herbs and half the garlic. Add salt and pepper to taste. Beat well. In a separate bowl, whisk the egg whites to a soft peak, then fold into the cheese mixture until they are evenly incorporated.

3 Preheat the oven to 180°C/ 350°F/Gas 4. Line the base of a lightly oiled 900g/2lb loaf tin. Put one-third of the cheese mixture in the tin and spread level. Arrange half the pepper strips on top in an even layer. Repeat until all the cheese and peppers are used, ending with a layer of the cheese mixture.

4 Cover the tin with foil and place in a roasting tin. Pour in boiling water to come halfway up the sides of the tin. Bake for 1 hour. Leave to cool in the water bath, then lift out and chill overnight.

5 A few hours before serving, make the salsa. Place the remaining skinned pepper and fresh peppers in a food processor. Add the remaining garlic, oil and vinegar. Set aside a few basil leaves for garnishing and add the rest to the processor. Process until finely chopped. Tip the mixture into a bowl, add salt and pepper to taste and mix well. Cover and chill until ready to serve.

6 Turn out the terrine, peel off the lining paper and slice thickly. Garnish with the reserved basil leaves and serve cold, with the sweet pepper salsa.

Asparagus and Egg Terrine

For a special dinner this terrine is a delicious choice yet it is very light. Make the hollandaise sauce well in advance and warm through gently when required.

Serves 8

150ml/¼ pint/⅔ cup milk

150ml/¼ pint/⅔ cup double cream

40g/1½oz/3 tbsp butter

40g/1½oz/3 tbsp flour

75g/3oz herbed or garlic cream cheese

675g/1½ lb asparagus spears, cooked

a little oil

2 eggs, separated

15ml/1 tbsp snipped fresh chives

30ml/2 tbsp chopped fresh dill

salt and ground black pepper

dill sprigs, to garnish

For the orange hollandaise sauce

15ml/1 tbsp white wine vinegar

15ml/1 tbsp fresh orange juice

4 black peppercorns

1 bay leaf

2 egg yolks

115g/4oz/½ cup butter, melted and cooled slightly

1 Put the milk and cream into a small saucepan and heat to just below boiling point. Melt the butter in a medium pan, stir in the flour and cook to a thick paste. Gradually stir in the milk, whisking as it thickens and beat to a smooth paste. Stir in the cream cheese, season to taste with salt and ground black pepper and leave to cool slightly.

2 Trim the asparagus to fit the width of a 1.2 litre/2 pint/ 5 cup bread tin or terrine. Lightly oil the tin and then place a sheet of greaseproof paper in the base, cut to fit. Preheat the oven to 180°C/ 350°F/Gas 4.

3 Beat the yolks into the sauce mixture. Whisk the whites until stiff and fold in with the chives, dill and seasoning. Layer the asparagus and egg mixture in the tin, starting and finishing with asparagus. Cover the top with foil.

4 Place the terrine in a roasting tin; half fill with hot water. Cook for 45–55 minutes until firm.

5 To make the sauce, put the vinegar, juice, peppercorns and bay leaf in a small pan and heat until reduced by half.

6 Cool the sauce slightly, then whisk in the egg yolks, then the butter, with a balloon whisk over a very gentle heat. Season to taste and keep whisking until thick. Keep the sauce warm over a pan of hot water.

7 When the terrine is just firm to the touch remove from the oven and allow to cool, then chill. Carefully invert the terrine on to a serving dish, remove the grease-proof paper and garnish with the dill. Cut into slices and pour over the warmed sauce.

Haddock and Smoked Salmon Terrine

This is a fairly substantial terrine so serve modest slices, perhaps accompanied by fresh dill mayonnaise or a fresh mango salsa. Follow with a light main course and a fruit-based dessert.

INGREDIENTS

Serves 10–12

15ml/1 tbsp sunflower oil,
    for greasing
350g/12oz oak-smoked salmon
900g/2lb haddock fillets, skinned
2 eggs, lightly beaten
105ml/7 tbsp crème fraîche
30ml/2 tbsp drained capers
30ml/2 tbsp drained soft green or
    pink peppercorns
salt and ground white pepper
crème fraîche, peppercorns and fresh dill
    and rocket, to garnish

1 Preheat the oven to 200°C/ 400°F/Gas 6. Grease a 1 litre/ 1¾ pint/4 cup loaf tin or terrine with the sunflower oil. Use some of the smoked salmon to line the loaf tin or terrine, allowing some of the ends to overhang the mould. Reserve the remaining smoked salmon until needed.

2 Cut two long slices of haddock the length of the tin or terrine and set aside. Cut the rest of the haddock into small pieces. Season all of the haddock with salt and ground white pepper.

3 Combine the eggs, crème fraîche, capers and green or pink peppercorns in a bowl. Add salt and pepper; stir in the haddock pieces. Spoon the mixture into the mould until it is one-third full. Smooth the surface with a spatula.

4 Wrap the long haddock fillets in the reserved salmon. Lay them on top of the layer of the fish mixture in the tin or terrine.

5 Cover with the rest of the fish mixture, smooth the surface and fold the overhanging pieces of salmon over the top. Cover tightly with a double thickness of foil. Tap the terrine to settle the contents.

6 Stand the terrine in a roasting tin and pour in boiling water to come halfway up the sides. Place in the oven and cook for 45 minutes–1 hour, until the filling is just set.

7 Take the terrine out of the roasting tin, but do not remove the foil cover. Place two or three large heavy tins on the foil to weight it and leave until cold. Chill in the fridge for 24 hours.

8 About an hour before serving, remove the terrine from the fridge, lift off the weights and remove the foil. Carefully invert on to a serving plate and garnish with crème fraîche, peppercorns and sprigs of dill and rocket leaves.

COOK'S TIP

Use any thick white fish fillets for this terrine; try cod, whiting, hake or hoki.

Turkey, Juniper and Peppercorn Terrine

This is an ideal dish for entertaining, as it can be made several days in advance. If you prefer, arrange some of the pancetta and pistachio nuts as a layer in the middle of the terrine.

INGREDIENTS

Serves 10–12

225g/8oz chicken livers, trimmed

450g/1lb minced turkey

450g/11b minced pork

225g/8oz cubetti pancetta

50g/2oz/½ cup shelled pistachio nuts, roughly chopped

5ml/1 tsp salt

2.5ml/½ tsp ground mace

2 garlic cloves, crushed

5ml/1 tsp drained green peppercorns in brine

5ml/1 tsp juniper berries

120ml/4fl oz/½ cup dry white wine

30ml/2 tbsp gin

finely grated rind of 1 orange

8 large vacuum-packed vine leaves in brine

oil, for greasing

1 Chop the chicken livers finely. Put them in a bowl and add the turkey, pork, pancetta, pistachio nuts, salt, mace and garlic. Mix well.

2 Lightly crush the peppercorns and juniper berries and add them to the mixture. Stir in the white wine, gin and orange rind. Cover and chill overnight to allow the flavours to mingle.

3 Preheat the oven to 160°C/ 325°F/Gas 3. Rinse the vine leaves under cold running water. Drain them thoroughly. Lightly oil a 1.2 litre/2 pint/5 cup pâté terrine or loaf tin. Line the terrine or tin with the leaves, letting the ends hang over the sides. Pack the mixture into the terrine or tin and fold the leaves over to enclose the filling. Brush lightly with oil.

4 Cover the terrine with its lid or with foil. Place it in a roasting tin and pour in boiling water to come halfway up the sides of the terrine. Bake for 1¾ hours, checking the level of the water occasionally, so that the roasting tin does not dry out.

5 Leave the terrine to cool, then pour off the surface juices. Cover with clear film, then foil and place weights on top. Chill in the fridge overnight. Serve at room temperature with a pickle or chutney such as spiced kumquats or red pepper and chilli jelly.

Chicken and Pork Terrine

This pale, elegant terrine is flecked with green peppercorns and parsley which give it a wonderfully subtle flavour.

INGREDIENTS

Serves 6–8

225g/8oz rindless, streaky bacon
375g/13oz boneless chicken breast, skinned
15ml/1 tbsp lemon juice
225g/8oz lean minced pork
½ small onion, finely chopped
2 eggs, beaten
30ml/2 tbsp chopped fresh parsley
5ml/1 tsp salt
5ml/1 tsp green peppercorns, crushed
oil, for greasing
salad leaves, radishes and lemon wedges, to serve

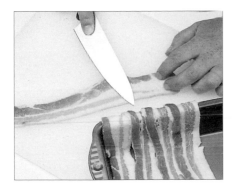

1 Preheat the oven to 160°C/ 325°F/Gas 3. Put the bacon on a board and stretch it using the back of a knife before arranging it in overlapping slices over the base and sides of a 900g/2lb loaf tin.

2 Cut 115g/4oz of the chicken into strips about 10cm/4in long. Sprinkle with lemon juice. Put the rest of the chicken in a food processor or blender with the minced pork and the onion. Process until fairly smooth.

3 Add the eggs, parsley, salt and peppercorns to the meat mixture and process again briefly. Spoon half the mixture into the loaf tin and then level the surface.

4 Arrange the chicken strips on top, then spoon in the remaining meat mixture and smooth the top. Give the tin a couple of sharp taps to knock out any pockets of air.

5 Cover the loaf tin with a piece of oiled foil and put it in a roasting tin. Pour in enough hot water to come halfway up the sides of the loaf tin. Bake for about 45–50 minutes, until firm.

6 Allow the terrine to cool in the tin before turning out and chilling. Serve sliced, with salad leaves, radishes and wedges of lemon for squeezing.

COOK'S TIP

For a slightly sharper flavour, substitute chopped fresh coriander for the parsley. It goes well with the lemon.

Twice-baked Gruyère and Potato Soufflé

A great starter dish, this recipe can be prepared in advance if you are entertaining and given its second baking just before you serve it up.

INGREDIENTS

Serves 4

225g/8oz floury potatoes

2 eggs, separated

175g/6oz/1½ cups Gruyère, grated

50g/2oz/½ cup self-raising flour

50g/2oz spinach leaves

butter, for greasing

salt and ground black pepper

salad leaves, to serve

3 Finely chop the spinach and fold into the potato mixture.

4 Whip the egg whites until they form soft peaks. Fold a little of the egg white into the mixture to slacken it slightly. Using a large spoon, fold the remaining egg white into the mixture.

5 Grease 4 large ramekin dishes. Pour the mixture into the dishes; place on a baking sheet. Bake for 20 minutes. Remove from the oven and allow to cool.

6 Turn the soufflés out on to a baking sheet and scatter with the remaining cheese. Bake again for 5 minutes; serve with salad leaves.

1 Preheat the oven to 200°C/ 400°F/Gas 6. Peel the potatoes and cook in lightly salted boiling water for 20 minutes until very tender. Drain and mash with the egg yolks.

2 Stir in half of the Gruyère cheese and all of the flour. Season to taste with salt and ground black pepper.

VARIATION

For a different flavouring try replacing the Gruyère with a crumbled blue cheese, such as Stilton or Shropshire Blue, which have a stronger taste.

Hot Crab Soufflés

These delicious little soufflés must be served as soon as they are ready, so seat your guests at the table before taking the soufflés out of the oven.

INGREDIENTS

Serves 6

50g/2oz/¼ cup butter

45ml/3 tbsp fine wholemeal breadcrumbs

4 spring onions, finely chopped

15ml/1 tbsp Malayan or mild Madras curry powder

25g/1oz/2 tbsp plain flour

105ml/7 tbsp coconut milk or milk

150ml/¼ pint/⅔ cup whipping cream

4 egg yolks

225g/8oz white crab meat

mild green Tabasco sauce

6 egg whites

salt and ground black pepper

1 Use some of the butter to grease six ramekin dishes or a 1.75 litre/3 pint/7½ cup soufflé dish. Sprinkle in the fine wholemeal breadcrumbs, roll the dishes or dish around to coat the base and sides completely, then tip out the excess breadcrumbs. Preheat the oven to 200°C/400°F/Gas 6.

2 Melt the remaining butter in a saucepan, add the spring onions and Malayan or mild Madras curry powder and cook over a low heat for about 1 minute, until softened. Stir in the flour and cook for a further 1 minute.

3 Gradually add the coconut milk or milk and the cream, stirring constantly. Cook until smooth and thick. Off the heat, stir in the egg yolks, then the crab. Season with salt, black pepper and Tabasco sauce.

4 In a grease-free bowl, beat the egg whites stiffly with a pinch of salt. With a metal spoon stir one-third into the crab mixture then fold in the rest. Spoon into the dishes or dish.

5 Bake until well risen, golden brown and just firm to the touch. Individual soufflés will take 8 minutes; a large soufflé will take 15–20 minutes. Serve at once.

Pastries, Tartlets & Toasts

Nothing compares with the taste of home-made, buttery pastry; few things are as impressive as a dainty filo pastry cup filled with prawns, and until you've tried a simple starter of cannellini beans and fruity olive oil on crispy bruschetta you won't know what you're missing.

Garlic Prawns in Filo Tartlets

Tartlets made with crisp layers of filo pastry and filled with garlic prawns make a tempting starter.

INGREDIENTS

Serves 4
For the tartlets
50g/2oz/4 tbsp butter, melted
2–3 large sheets filo pastry

For the filling
115g/4oz/½ cup butter
2–3 garlic cloves, crushed
1 red chilli, seeded and chopped
350g/12oz/3 cups cooked peeled prawns
30ml/2 tbsp chopped fresh parsley or
   snipped fresh chives
salt and ground black pepper

1 Preheat the oven to 200°C/ 400°F/Gas 6. Brush four individual 7.5cm/3in flan tins with melted butter.

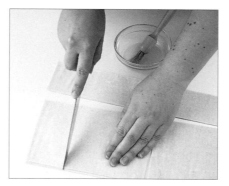

2 Cut the filo pastry into twelve 10cm/4in squares and brush with the melted butter.

3 Place three squares inside each tin, overlapping them at slight angles and carefully frilling the edges and points while forming a good hollow in each centre. Bake in the oven for 10–15 minutes, until crisp and golden. Leave to cool slightly then remove the pastry cases from the tins.

4 Meanwhile, make the filling. Melt the butter in a large frying pan, then add the garlic, chilli and prawns and fry quickly for 1–2 minutes to warm through. Stir in the fresh parsley or chives and season with salt and plenty of black pepper.

5 Spoon the prawn filling into the tartlets and serve at once, perhaps with some soured cream.

Crab and Ricotta Tartlets

Use the meat from a freshly cooked crab, weighing about 450g/1lb, if you can. Otherwise, look out for frozen brown and white crabmeat.

INGREDIENTS

Serves 4

225g/8oz/2 cups plain flour

pinch of salt

115g/4oz/½ cup butter, diced

225g/8oz/1 cup ricotta

15ml/1 tbsp grated onion

30ml/2 tbsp freshly grated
  Parmesan cheese

2.5ml/½ tsp mustard powder

2 eggs, plus 1 egg yolk

225g/8oz crabmeat

30ml/2 tbsp chopped fresh parsley

2.5–5ml/½–1 tsp anchovy essence

5–10ml/1–2 tsp lemon juice

salt and cayenne pepper

salad leaves, to garnish

1 Preheat the oven to 200°C/400°F/Gas 6. Sift the flour and salt into a bowl, add the butter and rub it in until the mixture resembles fine bread-crumbs. Stir in about 60ml/4 tbsp cold water to make a firm dough.

2 Turn the dough on to a floured surface and knead lightly. Roll out the pastry and use to line four 10cm/4in tartlet tins. Prick the bases with a fork, then chill for 30 minutes.

3 Line the pastry cases with grease-proof paper and fill with baking beans. Bake for 10 minutes, then remove the paper and beans. Return to the oven and bake for a further 10 minutes.

4 Place the ricotta, grated onion, Parmesan and mustard powder in a bowl and beat until soft. Gradually beat in the eggs and egg yolk.

5 Gently stir in the crabmeat and chopped parsley, then add the anchovy essence, lemon juice, salt and cayenne pepper, to taste.

6 Remove the tartlet cases from the oven and reduce the temperature to 180°C/350°F/Gas 4. Spoon the filling into the cases and bake for 20 minutes, until set and golden brown. Serve hot with a garnish of salad leaves.

Tiger Prawns with Mint, Dill and Lime

A wonderful combination – mint, dill and lime blend together to make a magical concoction to flavour succulent tiger prawns that will delight everyone who tries it.

INGREDIENTS

Serves 4

4 large sheets filo pastry

75g/3oz/⅓ cup butter

16 large tiger prawns, cooked and peeled

15ml/1 tbsp chopped fresh mint, plus
   extra to garnish

15ml/1 tbsp chopped fresh dill

juice of 1 lime

8 cooked unpeeled tiger prawns and
   lime wedges, to serve

1 Keep the sheets of filo pastry covered with a dry, clean cloth to keep them moist. Cut one sheet of filo pastry in half widthways and brush with melted butter. Place one half on top of the other.

2 Preheat the oven to 230°C/ 450°F/Gas 8. Cut the tiger prawns in half down the back of the prawn and remove the dark vein.

3 Place four prawns in the centre of the filo pastry and sprinkle a quarter of the mint, dill and lime juice over the top. Fold over the sides, brush with butter and roll up to make a parcel.

4 Once you have filled all the parcels place them join side down, on a greased baking sheet. Bake for 10 minutes or until golden. Serve with whole tiger prawns, lime wedges and mint.

Wild Mushroom and Fontina Tarts

Italian fontina cheese gives these tarts a creamy, nutty flavour. Serve them warm with rocket leaves.

INGREDIENTS

Serves 4

25g/1oz/½ cup dried wild mushrooms
30ml/2 tbsp olive oil
1 red onion, chopped
2 garlic cloves, chopped
30ml/2 tbsp medium-dry sherry
1 egg
120ml/4fl oz/½ cup single cream
25g/1oz fontina cheese, thinly sliced
salt and ground black pepper
rocket leaves, to serve

For the pastry

115g/4oz/1 cup wholemeal flour
50g/2oz/4 tbsp unsalted butter
25g/1oz/¼ cup walnuts, roasted
   and ground
1 egg, lightly beaten

1 To make the pastry, rub the flour and butter together until the mixture resembles fine breadcrumbs. Add the nuts then the egg; mix to a soft dough. Wrap, then chill for 30 minutes.

2 Meanwhile, soak the dried wild mushrooms in 300ml/ ½ pint/1¼ cups boiling water for 30 minutes. Drain and reserve the liquid. Fry the onion in the oil for 5 minutes, then add the garlic and fry for about 2 minutes, stirring.

3 Add the soaked mushrooms and cook for 7 minutes over a high heat until the edges become crisp. Add the sherry and the reserved liquid. Cook over a high heat for about 10 minutes until the liquid evaporates. Season and set aside to cool.

COOK'S TIP

You can prepare the pastry cases in advance, bake them blind for 10 minutes, then store in an airtight container for up to 2 days.

4 Preheat the oven to 200°C/400°F/Gas 6. Lightly grease four 10cm/4in tart tins. Roll out the pastry on a lightly floured work surface and use to line the tart tins.

5 Prick the pastry, line with greaseproof paper and baking beans and bake blind for about 10 minutes. Remove the paper and the beans.

6 Whisk the egg and cream to mix, add to the mushroom mixture, then season to taste. Spoon into the pastry cases, top with cheese slices and bake for 18 minutes until the filling is set. Serve warm with rocket.

Leek and Onion Tartlets

Baking in individual tins makes for easier serving for a starter and it looks attractive too. You could make tiny tartlets for parties.

INGREDIENTS

Serves 6

25g/1oz/2 tbsp butter

1 onion, thinly sliced

2.5ml/½ tsp dried thyme

450g/1lb leeks, thinly sliced

50g/2oz Gruyère or Emmenthal
    cheese, grated

3 eggs

300ml/½ pint/1¼ cups single cream

pinch of freshly grated nutmeg

salt and ground black pepper

mixed salad leaves, to serve

For the pastry

175g/6oz/1⅓ cup plain flour

75g/3oz/6 tbsp cold butter

1 egg yolk

30–45ml/2–3 tbsp cold water

2.5ml/½ tsp salt

1 To make the pastry, sift the flour into a bowl and add the butter. Using your fingertips, rub the butter into the flour until it resembles fine breadcrumbs. Make a well in the centre of the mixture.

2 Beat together the egg yolk, water and salt, pour into the well and combine the flour and liquid until it begins to stick together. Form into a ball. Wrap and chill for 30 minutes.

3 Butter six 10cm/4in tartlet tins. On a lightly floured surface, roll out the dough until 3mm/⅛in thick, then using a 12.5cm/5in cutter, cut as many rounds as possible. Gently ease the rounds into the tins, pressing the pastry firmly into the base and sides. Re-roll the trimmings and line the remaining tins. Prick the bases all over and chill in the fridge for 30 minutes.

4 Preheat the oven to 190°C/ 375°F/Gas 5. Line the pastry cases with foil and fill with baking beans. Place on a baking sheet and bake for 6–8 minutes until golden at the edges. Remove the foil and beans and bake for a further 2 minutes until the bases appear dry. Transfer to a wire rack to cool. Reduce the oven temperature to 180°C/350°F/Gas 4.

5 In a large frying pan, melt the butter over a medium heat, then add the onion and thyme and cook for 3–5 minutes until the onion is just softened, stirring frequently. Add the thinly sliced leeks and cook for 10–12 minutes until they are soft and tender, stirring occasionally. Divide the leek mixture among the pastry cases and sprinkle each with cheese, dividing it evenly.

6 In a medium bowl, beat the eggs, cream, nutmeg and salt and pepper. Place the pastry cases on a baking sheet and pour in the egg mixture. Bake for 15–20 minutes until set and golden. Transfer the tartlets to a wire rack to cool slightly, then remove them from the tins and serve warm or at room temperature with salad leaves.

Griddled Tomatoes on Soda Bread

Nothing could be simpler than this delightful appetizer, yet a drizzle of olive oil and balsamic vinegar and shavings of Parmesan cheese transform it into something really rather special.

INGREDIENTS

Serves 4

olive oil, for brushing and drizzling

6 tomatoes, thickly sliced

4 thick slices soda bread

balsamic vinegar, for drizzling

salt and ground black pepper

shavings of Parmesan cheese, to serve

1 Brush a griddle pan with olive oil and heat. Add the tomato slices and cook them for about 4 minutes, turning once, until softened and slightly blackened. Alternatively, heat the grill to high and line the rack with foil. Grill the tomato slices for 4–6 minutes, turning once, until softened.

2 Meanwhile, lightly toast the soda bread. Place the tomatoes on top of the toast and drizzle each portion with a little olive oil and balsamic vinegar. Season to taste and serve immediately with thin shavings of Parmesan cheese.

COOK'S TIP

Using a griddle pan reduces the amount of oil required for cooking the tomatoes which is useful for those watching their weight. It also gives them a delicious barbecued flavour.

Vegetable Tarte Tatin

This upside-down tart combines Mediterranean vegetables with rice, garlic, onions and olives.

INGREDIENTS

Serves 4

30ml/2 tbsp sunflower oil

about 25ml/1½ tbsp olive oil

1 aubergine, sliced lengthways

1 large red pepper, seeded and cut into
    long strips

5 tomatoes

2 red shallots, finely chopped

1–2 garlic cloves, crushed

150ml/¼ pint/⅔ cup white wine

10ml/2 tsp chopped fresh basil

225g/8oz/2 cups cooked white or brown
    long grain rice

40g/1½oz/⅔ cup stoned black
    olives, chopped

350g/12oz puff pastry, thawed if frozen

ground black pepper

salad leaves, to serve

1 Preheat the oven to 190°C/
375°F/Gas 5. Heat the
sunflower oil with 15ml/1 tbsp of
the olive oil and fry the aubergine
slices for 4–5 minutes on each side.
Drain on kitchen paper.

COOK'S TIP

Courgettes and mushrooms could
be used as well, or instead of, the
aubergines and peppers, or use
strips of lightly browned chicken.

---

2 Add the pepper strips to the oil
remaining in the pan, turning
them to coat. Cover the pan with a
lid or foil and sweat the peppers
over a moderately high heat for
5–6 minutes, stirring occasionally,
until the pepper strips are soft and
flecked with brown.

3 Slice two of the tomatoes and
set them aside. Plunge the
remaining tomatoes briefly into
boiling water, then peel them, cut
them into quarters and remove the
core and seeds. Chop the tomato
flesh roughly.

4 Heat the remaining oil in the
frying pan and fry the shallots
and garlic for 3–4 minutes until
softened. Then add the chopped
tomatoes and cook for a few
minutes until softened. Stir in the
wine and basil, with black pepper
to taste. Bring to the boil, then
remove from the heat and stir in
the cooked rice and black olives.

5 Arrange the tomato slices,
aubergine slices and peppers
in a single layer on the base of a
heavy, 30cm/12in, shallow
ovenproof dish. Spread the rice
mixture on top.

6 Roll out the pastry to a circle
slightly larger than the
diameter of the dish and place on
top of the rice, tucking the overlap
down inside the dish.

7 Bake for 25–30 minutes, until
the pastry is golden and risen.
Cool slightly, then invert the tart
on to a large, warmed serving
plate. Serve in slices, with some
salad leaves.

Greek Aubergine and Spinach Pie

Aubergines layered with spinach, feta cheese and rice make a flavoursome and dramatic filling for a pie. It can be served warm or cold in elegant slices.

INGREDIENTS

Serves 12

375g/13oz shortcrust pastry, thawed
   if frozen
45–60ml/3–4 tbsp olive oil
1 large aubergine, sliced into rounds
1 onion, chopped
1 garlic clove, crushed
175g/6oz spinach, washed
4 eggs
75g/3oz/½ cup crumbled feta cheese
40g/1½oz/½ cup freshly grated
   Parmesan cheese
60ml/4 tbsp natural yogurt
90ml/6 tbsp creamy milk
225g/8oz/2 cups cooked white or brown
   long grain rice
salt and ground black pepper

2 Heat 30–45ml/2–3 tbsp of the oil in a frying pan and fry the aubergine slices for 6–8 minutes on each side until golden. You may need to add a little more oil at first, but this will be released as the flesh softens. Lift out and drain well on kitchen paper.

3 Add the onion and garlic to the oil remaining in the pan then fry over a gentle heat for 4–5 minutes until soft, adding a little extra oil if necessary.

5 Spread the rice in an even layer over the base of the part-baked pastry case. Reserve a few aubergine slices for the top, and arrange the rest in an even layer over the rice.

6 Spoon the spinach and feta mixture over the aubergines and place the remaining slices on top. Bake for 30–40 minutes until lightly browned. Serve the pie while warm, or leave it to cool completely before transferring to a serving plate.

1 Preheat the oven to 180°C/ 350°F/Gas 4. Roll out the pastry thinly and use to line a 25cm/10in flan tin. Prick the base all over and bake in the oven for 10–12 minutes until the pastry is pale golden. (Alternatively, bake blind, having lined the pastry with baking parchment and weighted it with a handful of baking beans.)

4 Chop the spinach finely, by hand or in a food processor. Beat the eggs in a large mixing bowl, then add the spinach, feta, Parmesan, yogurt, milk and the onion mixture. Season well with salt and ground black pepper and stir thoroughly to mix.

COOK'S TIP

Courgettes could be used in place of the aubergines, if you prefer. Fry the sliced courgettes in a little oil for 3–4 minutes until they are evenly golden. You will need to use three to four standard courgettes, or choose baby courgettes instead and slice them horizontally.

Egg and Salmon Puff Parcels

These crisp elegant parcels hide a mouthwatering collection of flavours and textures and make a delicious starter or lunch dish.

INGREDIENTS

Serves 6

75g/3oz/scant ½ cup long grain rice
300ml/½ pint/1¼ cups fish stock
350g/12oz piece salmon tail
juice of ½ lemon
15ml/1 tbsp chopped fresh dill
15ml/1 tbsp chopped fresh parsley
10ml/2 tsp mild curry powder
6 small eggs, soft-boiled and cooled
425g/15oz flaky pastry, thawed if frozen
1 small egg, beaten
salt and ground black pepper

1 Cook the rice in the fish stock according to the packet's instructions, then drain and set aside to cool. Preheat the oven to 220°C/425°F/Gas 7.

2 Poach the salmon, then remove the bones and skin and flake the fish into the rice. Add the lemon juice, herbs, curry powder and seasoning and mix well. Peel the eggs.

COOK'S TIP

You can also add a spoonful of cooked chopped fresh or frozen spinach to each parcel.

3 Roll out the pastry and cut into six 14–15cm/5½–6in squares. Brush the edges with the beaten egg. Place a spoonful of rice in the middle of each square, push an egg into the middle and top with a little more rice.

4 Pull over the pastry corners to the middle to form a square parcel, squeezing the joins together well to seal. Brush with more egg, place on a baking sheet and bake the puffs for 20 minutes, then reduce the oven temperature to 190°C/375°F/Gas 5 and cook the puffs for a further 10 minutes or until golden and crisp underneath.

5 Cool slightly before serving, with a curry flavoured mayonnaise or Hollandaise sauce, if you like.

Thai-style Seafood Pasties

These elegant appetizer-size pasties are filled with fish, prawns and Thai fragrant rice, and are subtly flavoured with fresh coriander, garlic and ginger.

INGREDIENTS

Makes 18

plain flour, for dusting

500g/1¼lb puff pastry, thawed if frozen

1 egg, beaten with 30ml/2 tbsp water

lime twists, to garnish

For the filling

275g/10oz skinned white fish fillets, such as cod or haddock

seasoned plain flour

8–10 large raw prawns

15ml/1 tbsp sunflower oil

about 75g/3oz/6 tbsp butter

6 spring onions, finely sliced

1 garlic clove, crushed

225g/8oz/2 cups cooked Thai fragrant rice

4cm/1½ in piece fresh root ginger, grated

10ml/2 tsp finely chopped fresh coriander

5ml/1 tsp finely grated lime rind

1 Preheat the oven to 190°C/375°F/Gas 5. Make the filling. Cut the fish into 2cm/¾in cubes and dust with seasoned flour. Peel and devein the prawns and cut each one into four pieces.

2 Heat half of the oil and 15g/½oz/1 tbsp of the butter in a frying pan. Fry the spring onions gently for 2 minutes.

3 Add the garlic and fry for a further 5 minutes, until the onions are very soft. Transfer to a large bowl.

4 Heat the remaining oil and a further 25g/1oz/2 tbsp of the butter in a clean pan. Fry the fish pieces briefly. As soon as they begin to turn opaque, use a slotted spoon to transfer them to the bowl with the spring onions. Cook the prawns in the fat remaining in the pan. When they begin to change colour, lift them out and add them to the bowl.

5 Add the cooked rice to the bowl, with the fresh root ginger, coriander and grated lime rind. Mix, taking care not to break up the fish.

6 Dust the work surface with a little flour. Roll out the pastry and cut into 10cm/4in rounds. Place spoonfuls of filling just off centre on the pastry rounds. Dot with a little of the remaining butter. Dampen the edges of the pastry with a little of the egg wash, fold one side of the pastry over the filling and press the edges together firmly.

7 Place the pasties on two lightly greased baking sheets. Decorate them with the pastry trimmings, if you like, and brush them with egg wash. Bake in the oven for 12–15 minutes or until golden brown all over.

8 Transfer to a plate and garnish with lime twists.

Marinated Feta Cheese with Capers

Marinating cubes of feta cheese with herbs and spices gives a marvellous flavour. Serve with toast.

INGREDIENTS

Serves 6

350g/12oz feta cheese

2 garlic cloves

2.5ml/½ tsp mixed peppercorns

8 coriander seeds

1 bay leaf

15–30ml/1–2 tbsp drained capers

oregano or thyme sprigs

olive oil, to cover

hot toast, to serve

1 Cut the feta cheese into cubes. Thickly slice the garlic. Put the mixed peppercorns and coriander seeds in a mortar and crush lightly with a pestle.

2 Pack the feta cubes into a large preserving jar with the bay leaf, interspersing layers of cheese with garlic, crushed peppercorns and coriander, capers and the fresh oregano or thyme sprigs.

3 Pour in enough olive oil to cover the cheese. Close tightly and leave to marinate for two weeks in the fridge.

4 Lift out the feta cubes and serve on hot toast, with some chopped tomatoes and a little of the flavoured oil from the jar drizzled over.

COOK'S TIP

Add stoned black or green olives to the feta cheese in the marinade if you like.

Cannellini Bean and Rosemary Bruschetta

This variation on the theme of beans on toast makes an unusual but sophisticated starter.

INGREDIENTS

Serves 6

150g/5oz/⅔ cup dried cannellini beans

5 tomatoes

45ml/3 tbsp olive oil, plus extra
   for drizzling

2 sun-dried tomatoes in oil, drained and
   finely chopped

1 garlic clove, crushed

30ml/2 tbsp chopped fresh rosemary

12 slices Italian-style bread, such
   as ciabatta

1 large garlic clove

salt and ground black pepper

handful of fresh basil leaves, to garnish

1 Put the beans in a bowl, cover in water and soak overnight. Drain and rinse the beans, then place in a saucepan and cover with fresh water. Bring to the boil and boil rapidly for 10 minutes. Then simmer for 50–60 minutes or until tender. Drain, return to the pan and keep warm.

2 Meanwhile, place the tomatoes in a bowl, cover with boiling water; leave for 30 seconds, then peel, seed and chop the flesh. Heat the oil in a frying pan, add the fresh and sun-dried tomatoes, garlic and rosemary. Cook for 2 minutes until the tomatoes begin to break down and soften.

3 Add the tomato mixture to the cannellini beans and season to taste. Mix together well. Keep the bean mixture warm.

4 Rub the cut sides of the bread slices with the garlic clove, then toast them lightly. Spoon the cannellini bean mixture on top of the toast. Sprinkle with basil leaves and drizzle with a little extra olive oil before serving.

Fish, Meat & Poultry

What can match the memorable taste of a properly made Prawn Cocktail? Perhaps only Grilled Scallops with Brown Butter, or asparagus wrapped in salt-cured ham. Whatever your preferences there are fish, meat and poultry recipes here to suit all tastes and appetites.

Prawn Cocktail

There is no nicer starter than a good, fresh prawn cocktail – and nothing nastier than one in which soggy prawns swim in a thin, vinegary sauce embedded in limp lettuce. This recipe shows just how good a prawn cocktail can be.

INGREDIENTS

Serves 6

60ml/4 tbsp double cream, lightly
    whipped
60ml/4 tbsp mayonnaise, preferably
    home-made
60ml/4 tbsp tomato ketchup
5–10ml/1–2 tsp Worcestershire sauce
juice of 1 lemon
½ cos lettuce or other very crisp lettuce
450g/1lb/4 cups cooked peeled prawns
salt, ground black pepper and paprika
6 large whole cooked unpeeled prawns,
    to garnish (optional)
thinly sliced brown bread and lemon
    wedges, to serve

1 In a bowl, mix together the whipped cream, mayonnaise and ketchup. Add Worcestershire sauce to taste. Stir in enough lemon juice to make a really tangy cocktail sauce.

2 Finely shred the lettuce and fill six individual glasses one-third full. Stir the prawns into the sauce, then check the seasoning. Spoon the prawn mixture generously over the lettuce.

3 If you like, drape a whole cooked prawn over the edge of each glass (see Cook's Tip). Sprinkle each of the cocktails with ground black pepper and some paprika. Serve immediately, with thinly sliced brown bread and butter and lemon wedges for squeezing over.

COOK'S TIP
~

To prepare the garnish, peel the body shell from the prawns and leave the tail "fan" for decoration.

Marinated Asparagus and Langoustine

For a really extravagant treat, you could make this attractive salad with medallions of lobster. For a cheaper version, use large prawns, allowing six per serving.

INGREDIENTS

Serves 4

16 langoustines

16 fresh asparagus spears, trimmed

2 carrots

30ml/2 tbsp olive oil

1 garlic clove, peeled

salt and ground black pepper

4 fresh tarragon sprigs and some chopped, to garnish

For the dressing

30ml/2 tbsp tarragon vinegar

120ml/4fl oz/½ cup olive oil

1 Peel the langoustines and keep the discarded parts for stock. Set aside.

2 Steam the asparagus over boiling salted water until just tender, but still a little crisp. Refresh under cold water, drain and place in a shallow dish.

3 Peel the carrots and cut into fine julienne shreds. Cook in a pan of lightly salted boiling water for about 3 minutes, until tender but still crunchy. Drain, refresh under cold water, drain again. Add to the asparagus.

4 Make the dressing. In a jug, whisk the tarragon vinegar with the oil. Season to taste. Pour over the asparagus and carrots and leave to marinate.

5 Heat the oil with the garlic in a frying pan until very hot. Add the langoustines and sauté quickly until just heated through. Discard the garlic.

6 Arrange four asparagus spears and the carrots on four individual plates. Drizzle over the dressing left in the dish and top each portion with four langoustine tails. Top with the tarragon sprigs and scatter the chopped tarragon on top. Serve immediately.

COOK'S TIP

Most of the langoustines we buy have been cooked at sea, a necessary act because the flesh deteriorates rapidly after death. Bear this in mind when you cook the shellfish. Because it has already been cooked, it will only need to be lightly sautéed until heated through. If you are lucky enough to buy live langoustines, kill them quickly by immersing them in boiling water, then sauté until cooked through.

Clams with Chilli and Yellow Bean Sauce

This delicious Thai-inspired dish is simple to prepare. It can be made in a matter of minutes so will not keep you away from your guests for very long.

INGREDIENTS

Serves 4–6

1kg/2¼ lb fresh clams

30ml/2 tbsp vegetable oil

4 garlic cloves, finely chopped

15ml/1 tbsp grated fresh root ginger

4 shallots, finely chopped

30ml/2 tbsp yellow bean sauce

6 red chillies, seeded and chopped

15ml/1 tbsp fish sauce

pinch of granulated sugar

handful of basil leaves, plus extra
   to garnish

1 Wash and scrub the clams. Heat the oil in a wok or large frying pan. Add the garlic and ginger and fry for 30 seconds, add the shallots and fry for a further minute.

2 Add the clams to the pan. Using a fish slice or spatula, turn them a few times to coat all over with the oil. Add the yellow bean sauce and half the chopped red chillies.

3 Continue to cook, stirring often, for 5–7 minutes, or until all the clams are open. You may need to add a splash of water. Adjust the seasoning with the fish sauce and a little sugar.

4 Finally add the basil leaves and stir to mix. Transfer the clams to individual bowls or a serving platter. Garnish with the remaining red chillies and basil leaves. Serve immediately.

Mussels and Clams with Lemon Grass

Lemon grass has an incomparable flavour and is excellent used with seafood. If you cannot find clams, use extra mussels instead.

INGREDIENTS

Serves 6

1.8–2kg/4–4½ lb mussels

450g/1lb baby clams, washed

120ml/4fl oz/½ cup dry white wine

1 bunch spring onions, chopped

2 lemon grass stalks, chopped

6 kaffir lime leaves, chopped

10ml/2 tsp Thai green curry paste

200ml/7fl oz/scant 1 cup coconut cream

30ml/2 tbsp chopped fresh coriander

salt and ground black pepper

whole garlic chives, to garnish

1 Clean the mussels. Pull off the beards and scrub the shells. Discard any that are broken or stay open when tapped.

2 Put the wine, spring onions, lemon grass, lime leaves and curry paste in a pan. Simmer until the wine almost evaporates.

3 Add the mussels and clams to the pan, cover tightly and steam the shellfish over a high heat for 5–6 minutes, until they open.

4 Using a slotted spoon, transfer the mussels and clams to a warmed serving bowl and keep hot. Discard any shellfish that remain closed. Strain the cooking liquid into a clean saucepan and then simmer to reduce the amount to about 250ml/8fl oz/1 cup.

5 Stir in the coconut cream and coriander, with salt and pepper to taste. Heat through. Pour over the seafood and serve, garnished with garlic chives.

COOK'S TIP

Buy a few extra mussels just in case there are any which have to be discarded.

Scallops Wrapped in Parma Ham

Cook these lovely skewers on the barbecue for al fresco *summer dining. Serve with lime wedges for a sharper flavour.*

INGREDIENTS

Serves 4

24 shucked medium-size scallops,
   corals removed
lemon juice
8–12 Parma ham slices, cut lengthways
   into 2 or 3 strips
olive oil, for brushing
ground black pepper
lemon wedges, to serve

1 Prepare the barbecue well in advance or preheat the grill when you make the skewers.

2 Sprinkle the scallops with lemon juice. Wrap a strip of Parma ham around each scallop. Thread on to 8 skewers.

3 Brush with oil. Arrange on a baking sheet if grilling. Grill about 10cm/4in from the heat, or cook over the barbecue, for 3–5 minutes on each side or until the scallops are opaque.

4 Set 2 skewers on each plate. Sprinkle the scallops with freshly ground black pepper and serve with lemon wedges.

COOK'S TIP

Use a short sturdy knife to pry shelled scallops open. Discard the membrane, organs and gristle at the side of the white meat. Set the coral aside. Rinse well.

Scallop-stuffed Roast Peppers with Pesto

Serve these scallop-and-pesto-filled sweet red peppers with Italian bread, such as ciabatta or focaccia, to mop up the garlicky juices.

INGREDIENTS

Serves 4

4 squat red peppers

2 large garlic cloves, cut into thin slivers

60ml/4 tbsp olive oil

4 shelled scallops

45ml/3 tbsp pesto sauce

salt and ground black pepper

freshly grated Parmesan cheese, to serve

salad leaves and basil sprigs, to garnish

1 Preheat the oven to 180°C/ 350°F/Gas 4. Cut the peppers in half lengthways, through their stalks. Scrape out and discard the cores and seeds. Wash the pepper shells and pat dry with kitchen paper.

2 Put the peppers, cut-side up, in an oiled roasting tin. Divide the slivers of garlic equally among them and sprinkle with salt and ground black pepper to taste. Then spoon the oil into the peppers and roast for 40 minutes.

3 Using a sharp knife, carefully cut each of the shelled scallops in half horizontally to make two flat discs each with a piece of coral. When cooked, remove the peppers from the oven and place a scallop half in each pepper half. Then top with the pesto sauce.

4 Return the tin to the oven and roast for 10 minutes more. Transfer the peppers to individual serving plates, sprinkle with grated Parmesan and garnish each plate with a few salad leaves and basil sprigs. Serve warm.

COOK'S TIP

Scallops are available from most fishmongers and supermarkets with fresh fish counters. Never cook scallops for longer than the time stated in the recipe or they will be tough and rubbery.

Grilled Scallops with Brown Butter

This is a very striking dish as the scallops are served on the half shell, still sizzling from the grill. Reserve it for a very special occasion.

Serves 4

50g/2oz/¼ cup unsalted butter, diced
8 scallops, prepared on the half shell
15ml/1 tbsp chopped fresh parsley
salt and ground black pepper
lemon wedges, to serve

COOK'S TIP

If you can't get hold of scallops in
their shells, you can use shelled,
fresh scallops if you cook them
on the day of purchase.

1 Preheat the grill to high. Melt the butter in a small saucepan over a medium heat until it is pale golden brown. Remove the pan from the heat immediately; the butter must not be allowed to burn. Arrange the scallop shells in a single layer in a casserole or a shallow roasting pan. Brush a little of the brown butter over them.

2 Grill the scallops for 4 minutes – it will not be necessary to turn them. Pour over the remaining brown butter, then sprinkle a little salt and pepper and the parsley over. Serve immediately, with lemon wedges for squeezing over.

Fried Squid

The squid is simply dusted in flour and dipped in egg before being fried, so the coating is light and does not mask the flavour.

Serves 2

115g/4oz prepared squid, cut into rings
30ml/2 tbsp seasoned plain flour
1 egg
30ml/2 tbsp milk
olive oil, for frying
sea salt, to taste
lemon wedges, to serve

COOK'S TIP

For a crisper coating, dust the
rings in flour, then dip them in
batter instead of this simple egg
and flour coating.

1 Toss the squid rings in the seasoned flour in a bowl or strong polythene bag. Beat the egg and milk together in a shallow bowl. Heat the oil in a heavy-based frying pan.

2 Dip the floured squid rings one at a time into the egg mixture, shaking off any excess liquid. Add to the hot oil, in batches if necessary, and fry for 2–3 minutes on each side until evenly golden all over.

3 Drain the fried squid on paper towels, then sprinkle with salt. Transfer to a small warm plate and serve with the lemon wedges.

Paella Croquettes

Paella is probably Spain's most famous dish, and here it is used for a tasty fried tapas. In this recipe, the paella is cooked from scratch, but you could, of course, use leftover paella instead.

INGREDIENTS

Serves 4
pinch of saffron threads
150ml/¼ pint/⅔ cup white wine
30ml/2 tbsp olive oil
1 small onion, finely chopped
1 garlic clove, finely chopped
150g/5oz/⅔ cup risotto rice
300ml/½ pint/1¼ cups hot chicken stock
50g/2oz /½ cup cooked prawns, peeled, deveined and coarsely chopped
50g/2oz cooked chicken, coarsely chopped
75g/3oz/⅔ cup petits pois, thawed if frozen
30ml/2 tbsp freshly grated Parmesan cheese
1 egg, beaten
30ml/2 tbsp milk
75g/3oz/1½ cups fresh white breadcrumbs
vegetable or olive oil, for shallow-frying
salt and ground black pepper
flat leaf parsley, to garnish

1 Stir the saffron into the wine in a small bowl; set aside.

2 Heat the oil in a saucepan and gently fry the onion and garlic for 5 minutes until softened. Stir in the risotto rice and cook, stirring, for 1 minute.

3 Keeping the heat fairly high, add the wine and saffron mixture to the pan, stirring until it is all absorbed. Gradually add the stock, stirring until all the liquid has been absorbed and the rice is cooked – this should take about 20 minutes.

4 Stir in the prawns, chicken, petits pois and freshly grated Parmesan. Season to taste. Leave to cool slightly, then use two tablespoons to shape the mixture into 16 small lozenges.

5 Mix the egg and milk in a shallow bowl. Spread out the breadcrumbs on a sheet of foil. Dip the croquettes in the egg mixture, then coat them evenly in the breadcrumbs.

6 Heat the oil in a large frying pan. Then shallow fry the croquettes for 4–5 minutes until crisp and golden brown. Work in batches. Drain on kitchen paper and keep hot. Serve garnished with a sprig of flat leaf parsley.

Smoked Salmon and Rice Salad Parcels

Feta, cucumber and tomatoes give a Greek flavour to the salad in these parcels, a combination which goes well with the rice, especially if a little wild rice is added.

INGREDIENTS

Serves 4

175g/6oz/scant 1 cup mixed wild rice and basmati rice

8 slices smoked salmon, total weight about 350g/12oz

10cm/4in piece of cucumber, finely diced

about 225g/8oz feta cheese, cubed

8 cherry tomatoes, quartered

30ml/2 tbsp mayonnaise

10ml/2 tsp fresh lime juice

15ml/1 tbsp chopped fresh chervil

salt and ground black pepper

lime slices and fresh chervil, to garnish

1 Cook the rice according to the instructions on the packet. Drain, tip into a bowl and leave to cool completely.

2 Line four ramekins with clear film, then line each ramekin with two slices of smoked salmon, allowing the ends to overlap the edges of the dishes.

COOK'S TIP
〜

Use smoked trout in place of the salmon if you wish.

---

3 Add the cucumber, feta and tomatoes to the rice, and stir in the mayonnaise, lime juice and chervil. Mix together well. Season with salt and ground black pepper to taste.

4 Spoon the rice mixture into the salmon-lined ramekins. (Any leftover mixture can be used to make a rice salad.) Then fold over the overlapping ends of salmon so that the rice mixture is completely encased.

5 Chill the parcels in the fridge for 30–60 minutes, then invert each parcel on to a plate, using the clear film to ease them out of the ramekins. Carefully peel off the clear film, then garnish each parcel with slices of lime and a sprig of fresh chervil and serve.

Monkfish Packages

Notoriously ugly, the monkfish makes delicious eating with its faintly shellfish-like flavour. You could use a cheaper fish but you'll lose that taste.

INGREDIENTS

Serves 4

175g/6oz/1½ cups bread flour

2 eggs

115g/4oz skinless monkfish fillet, diced

grated rind of 1 lemon

1 garlic clove, chopped

1 small red chilli, seeded and sliced

45ml/3 tbsp chopped fresh parsley

30ml/2 tbsp single cream

salt and ground black pepper

For the tomato oil

2 tomatoes, peeled, seeded and
   finely diced

45ml/3 tbsp extra virgin olive oil

15ml/1 tbsp lemon juice

1 Place the bread flour, eggs and 2.5ml/½ tsp salt in a blender or food processor; pulse until it forms a soft dough. Knead for 2–3 minutes. Wrap in clear film and chill for 20 minutes.

2 Place the monkfish, lemon rind, garlic, chilli and parsley in the clean food processor; process until very finely chopped. Add the cream, with plenty of salt and ground black pepper, and process again until a very thick paste is formed.

3 Make the tomato oil by stirring the diced tomatoes with the olive oil and lemon juice in a bowl. Add salt to taste. Cover and chill.

COOK'S TIP

~

If the dough is sticky, sprinkle a little flour into the bowl of the food processor.

---

4 Roll out the dough thinly on a lightly floured surface and cut out 32 rounds, using a 4cm/1½in plain cutter. Divide the filling among half the rounds, then cover with the remaining rounds. Pinch the edges tightly to seal, trying to exclude as much air as possible.

5 Bring a large saucepan of water to a simmer and poach the fish packages in batches, for 2–3 minutes, or until they rise to the surface. Drain and serve hot, drizzled with the tomato oil.

Three-colour Fish Kebabs

Don't leave the fish to marinate for more than an hour. The lemon juice will start to break down the fibres of the fish after this time and it will then be difficult to avoid overcooking it.

INGREDIENTS

Serves 4

120ml/4fl oz/½ cup olive oil

finely grated rind and juice of
1 large lemon

5ml/1 tsp crushed chilli flakes

350g/12oz monkfish fillet, cubed

350g/12oz swordfish fillet, cubed

350g/12oz thick salmon fillet or
steak, cubed

2 red, yellow or orange peppers, cored,
seeded and cut into squares

30ml/2 tbsp finely chopped fresh flat
leaf parsley

salt and ground black pepper

For the sweet tomato and chilli salsa

225g/8oz ripe tomatoes, finely chopped

1 garlic clove, crushed

1 fresh red chilli, seeded and chopped

45ml/3 tbsp extra virgin olive oil

15ml/1 tbsp lemon juice

15ml/1 tbsp finely chopped fresh flat
leaf parsley

pinch of sugar

1 Put the oil in a shallow glass or china bowl and add the lemon rind and juice, the chilli flakes and pepper to taste. Whisk to combine, then add the fish chunks. Turn to coat evenly.

2 Add the pepper squares, stir, then cover and marinate in a cool place for 1 hour, turning occasionally with a slotted spoon.

3 Thread the fish and peppers on to eight oiled metal skewers, reserving the marinade. Barbecue or grill the skewered fish for 5–8 minutes, turning once.

4 Meanwhile, make the salsa by mixing all the ingredients in a bowl, and seasoning to taste with salt and pepper. Heat the reserved marinade in a small pan, remove from the heat and stir in the parsley, with salt and pepper to taste. Serve the kebabs hot, with the marinade spooned over, accompanied by the salsa.

COOK'S TIP

Use tuna instead of swordfish, if you like. It has a similar meaty texture and will be equally successful.

Crab Cakes with Tartare Sauce

Sweet crab meat is offset by a piquant tartare sauce.

INGREDIENTS

Serves 4

675g/1½ lb fresh lump crab meat

1 egg, beaten

30ml/2 tbsp mayonnaise

15ml/1 tbsp Worcestershire sauce

15ml/1 tbsp sherry

30ml/2 tbsp minced fresh parsley

15ml/1 tbsp minced fresh chives or dill

salt and ground black pepper

45ml/3 tbsp olive oil

salad leaves, chives and lemon, to garnish

For the sauce

1 egg yolk

15ml/1 tbsp white wine vinegar

30ml/2 tbsp Dijon-style mustard

250ml/8fl oz/1 cup vegetable or
    groundnut oil

3ml/2 tbsp fresh lemon juice

60ml/4 tbsp minced spring onions

30ml/2 tbsp chopped drained capers

60ml/4 tbsp minced sour dill pickles

60ml/4 tbsp minced fresh parsley

1 Pick over the crab meat, removing any pieces of shell or cartilage. Keep the pieces of crab as large as possible.

2 In a mixing bowl, combine the beaten egg with the mayonnaise, Worcestershire sauce, sherry and herbs. Season with salt and lots of black pepper. Gently fold in the crab meat.

3 Divide the mixture into 8 portions and gently form each one into an oval cake. Place on a baking sheet between layers of greaseproof paper and chill for at least 1 hour.

4 Meanwhile, make the sauce. In a medium-size bowl, beat the egg yolk with a wire whisk until smooth. Add the vinegar, mustard, and salt and pepper to taste, and whisk for about 10 seconds to blend. Slowly whisk in the oil .

5 Add the lemon juice, spring onions, capers, pickles and parsley, and mix well. Check the seasoning. Cover and chill.

6 Preheat the grill. Brush the crab cakes with the olive oil. Place on an oiled baking sheet, in one layer.

7 Grill 15cm/6in from the heat until golden brown, about 5 minutes on each side. Serve the crab cakes with the tartare sauce, garnished with salad leaves, chives and lemon.

COOK'S TIP

For easier handling and to make the crab meat go further, add 50g/2oz/1 cup fresh breadcrumbs and 1 more egg to the crab mixture. Divide the mixture into 12 cakes to serve 6.

Salmon Cakes with Butter Sauce

Salmon fish cakes make a real treat for the start of a dinner party. They are also economical as you could use any small tail pieces which are on special offer from your local fishmonger or supermarket.

INGREDIENT

Makes 6

225g/8oz salmon tail piece, cooked

30ml/2 tbsp chopped fresh parsley

2 spring onions, trimmed and chopped

grated rind and juice of ½ lemon

225g/8oz mashed potato (not too soft)

1 egg, beaten

50g/2oz/1 cup fresh white breadcrumbs

75g/3oz/6 tbsp butter, plus extra for
    frying (optional)

oil, for frying (optional)

salt and ground black pepper

courgette and carrot slices and sprig of
    coriander, to garnish

1 Remove all the skin and bones from the fish and mash or flake it well. Add the fresh parsley, onions and 5ml/1 tsp of the lemon rind, and season with salt and lots of black pepper.

2 Gently work in the potato and then shape into six rounds, triangles or croquettes. Chill the salmon cakes for 20 minutes.

3 Preheat the grill. When chilled coat the salmon cakes well in egg and then in the breadcrumbs. Grill gently for 5 minutes on each side, or until they are golden, or fry in butter and oil.

4 To make the butter sauce, melt the butter, whisk in the remaining lemon rind, the lemon juice, 15–30ml/1–2 tbsp water and seasoning to taste. Simmer for a few minutes and serve with the hot fish cakes and garnish with slices of courgette and carrot and a sprig of coriander.

Breaded Sole Batons

Goujons of lemon sole are coated in seasoned flour and then in breadcrumbs, and fried until deliciously crispy. They are served with piquant tartare sauce.

Serves 4

275g/10oz lemon sole fillets, skinned
2 eggs
115g/4oz/1½ cups fine fresh breadcrumbs
75g/3oz/6 tbsp plain flour
salt and ground black pepper
vegetable oil, for frying
tartare sauce and lemon wedges, to serve

1 Cut the fish fillets into long diagonal strips about 2cm/¾in wide, using a sharp knife.

2 Break the eggs into a shallow dish and beat well with a fork. Place the breadcrumbs in another shallow dish. Put the flour in a large polythene bag and season with salt and plenty of ground black pepper.

3 Dip the fish strips in the egg, turning to coat well. Place on a plate and then taking a few at a time, shake them in the bag of flour. Dip the fish strips in the egg again, then in the breadcrumbs, turning to coat well. Place on a tray in a single layer, not touching. Let the coating set for at least 10 minutes.

4 Heat 1cm/½in oil in a large frying pan over a medium-high heat. When the oil is hot (a cube of bread will sizzle) fry the fish strips for about 2–2½ minutes in batches, turning once, taking care not to overcrowd the pan. Drain on kitchen paper and keep warm. Serve the fish with tartare sauce and lemon wedges.

Parmesan Fish Goujons

Use this batter, with or without the cheese, whenever you feel brave enough to fry fish. This is light and crisp, just like authentic fish-and-chip shop batter.

INGREDIENTS

Serves 4

375g/13oz plaice or sole fillets, or thicker
   fish such as cod or haddock
a little flour
oil, for deep-frying
salt and ground black pepper
dill sprigs, to garnish

For the cream sauce
60ml/4 tbsp soured cream
60ml/4 tbsp mayonnaise
2.5ml/$\frac{1}{2}$ tsp grated lemon rind
30ml/2 tbsp chopped gherkins or capers
15ml/1 tbsp chopped mixed fresh herbs,
   or 5ml/1 tsp dried

For the batter
75g/3oz/$\frac{3}{4}$ cup plain flour
25g/1oz/$\frac{1}{4}$ cup grated Parmesan cheese
5ml/1 tsp bicarbonate of soda
1 egg, separated
150ml/$\frac{1}{4}$ pint/$\frac{2}{3}$ cup milk

1 To make the cream sauce, mix
the soured cream, mayonnaise,
lemon rind, gherkins or capers,
herbs and seasoning together, then
place in the fridge to chill.

2 To make the batter, sift the
flour into a bowl. Mix in the
other dry ingredients and some
salt, and then whisk in the egg yolk
and milk to give a thick yet smooth
batter. Then gradually whisk in
90ml/6 tbsp water. Season and
place in the fridge to chill.

3 Skin the fish and cut into thin
strips of similar length. Season
the flour and then dip the fish
lightly in the flour.

4 Heat at least 5cm/2in oil in a
large pan with a lid. Whisk the
egg white until stiff and gently fold
into the batter until just blended.

5 Dip the floured fish into the
batter, drain off any excess and
then drop gently into the hot fat.

6 Cook the fish in batches so
that the goujons don't stick to
one another for only 3–4 minutes,
turning once. When the batter is
golden and crisp, remove the fish
with a slotted spoon. Place on
kitchen paper on a plate and keep
warm in a low oven while cooking
the remaining goujons.

7 Serve hot garnished with
sprigs of dill and accompanied
by the cream sauce.

Deep-fried Whitebait

A spicy coating on these fish gives this favourite dish a crunchy bite.

INGREDIENTS

Serves 6

115g/4oz/1 cup plain flour
2.5ml/½ tsp curry powder
2.5ml/½ tsp ground ginger
2.5ml/½ tsp ground cayenne pepper
pinch of salt
1.2kg/2½ lb whitebait, thawed if frozen
vegetable oil, for deep-frying
lemon wedges, to garnish

1 Mix together the plain flour, curry powder, ground ginger, cayenne pepper and a little salt in a large bowl.

2 Coat the fish in the seasoned flour, covering them evenly.

3 Heat the oil in a large, heavy-based saucepan until it reaches a temperature of 190°C/375°F. Fry the whitebait in batches for about 2–3 minutes until the fish is golden and crispy.

4 Drain the whitebait well on kitchen paper. Keep warm in a low oven until you have cooked all the fish. Serve at once garnished with lemon wedges for squeezing over.

Grilled Asparagus with Salt-cured Ham

Serve this tapas when asparagus is plentiful and not too expensive.

Serves 4

6 slices of Serrano ham

12 asparagus spears

15ml/1 tbsp olive oil

sea salt and coarsely ground black pepper

COOK'S TIP

If you can't find Serrano ham, use Italian prosciutto or Portuguese presunto.

1 Preheat the grill to high. Halve each slice of ham lengthways and wrap one half around each of the asparagus spears.

2 Brush the ham and asparagus lightly with oil and sprinkle with salt and pepper. Place on the grill rack. Grill for 5–6 minutes, turning frequently, until the asparagus is tender but still firm. Serve immediately.

Quail's Eggs in Aspic with Parma Ham

These clever looking eggs in jelly are so easy to make, and are great for summer eating. Serve them with salad leaves and some home-made mayonnaise on the side.

INGREDIENTS

Makes 12

22g packet aspic powder

45ml/3 tbsp dry sherry

12 quail's eggs

6 slices of Parma ham

12 fresh coriander or flat leaf
   parsley leaves

salad leaves, to serve

1 Make up the aspic following the packet instructions but replace 45ml/3 tbsp water with the dry sherry, giving a greater depth of flavour. Leave the aspic in the fridge until it begins to thicken, but not too thick.

2 Put the quail's eggs in a pan of cold water and bring to the boil. Boil for 1½ minutes only, then pour off the hot water and leave in cold water until cold. This way the yolks should still be a little soft but the whites will be firm enough to peel when really cold.

3 Rinse 12 dariole moulds so they are damp and place them on a tray. Cut the Parma ham into 12 pieces, then roll or fold so they will fit into the moulds.

4 Place a herb leaf in the base of each mould, then put a peeled egg on top. As the jelly begins to thicken pour in enough to nearly cover each egg, holding it steady. Then put the slice of ham on the egg and pour in the rest of the jelly to fill the mould, so that when you turn them out the eggs will be sitting on the ham.

5 Transfer the tray of moulds to a cold place and then leave for 3–4 hours until set and cold. When ready to serve run a knife around the top rim of the jelly to loosen. Dip the moulds into warm, not hot, water and shake or tap gently until they appear loose. Invert on to small plates and serve with salad leaves.

Chicken Bitki

This is a popular Polish dish and makes an attractive starter when offset by deep red beetroot and vibrant green salad leaves.

Makes 12

15g/½oz/1 tbsp butter, melted

115g/4oz flat mushrooms, finely chopped

50g/2oz/1 cup fresh white breadcrumbs

350g/12oz chicken breasts or guinea fowl, minced or finely chopped

2 eggs, separated

1.5ml/¼ tsp grated nutmeg

30ml/2 tbsp plain flour

45ml/3 tbsp oil

salt and ground black pepper

salad leaves and grated pickled beetroot, to serve

1 Melt the butter in a pan and fry the mushrooms for about 5 minutes until soft and the juices have evaporated. Allow to cool.

2 Mix the mushrooms and the breadcrumbs, the chicken or guinea fowl, egg yolks, nutmeg, salt and pepper together.

3 Whisk the egg whites until stiff. Stir half into the chicken mixture to slacken it, then fold in the remainder.

4 Shape into 12 even-size meatballs, about 7.5cm/3in long and 2.5cm/1in wide. Roll in the flour to coat.

5 Heat the oil in a frying pan and fry the bitki for about 10 minutes, turning until evenly golden brown and cooked through. Serve hot with salad leaves and pickled beetroot.

Five-spice Rib-sticker

*Choose the meatiest spare ribs you
can, to make these a real success.*

INGREDIENTS

Serves 8

1kg/2¼ lb pork spare ribs

10ml/2 tsp Chinese five-spice powder

2 garlic cloves, crushed

15ml/1 tbsp grated fresh root ginger

2.5ml/½ tsp chilli sauce

60ml/ 4 tbsp dark muscovado sugar

15ml/1 tbsp sunflower oil

4 spring onions

3 Cook the spare ribs under a
preheated medium-hot grill
turning frequently, for 30–40
minutes. Brush the ribs occasionally
with the remaining marinade.

4 While the ribs are cooking,
finely slice the spring onions –
on the diagonal. To serve, place the
ribs on a serving plate and scatter
the spring onions over the top.

1 If the spare ribs are still
attached together, cut between
them to separate them (or ask your
butcher to do this). Place the spare
ribs in a large bowl.

2 Mix together all the remaining
ingredients, except the spring
onions, and pour over the ribs.
Toss well to coat evenly. Cover the
bowl and leave to marinate in the
fridge overnight.

Stuffed Garlic Mushrooms with Prosciutto

Field mushrooms can vary greatly in size. Choose similar-size specimens with undamaged edges.

INGREDIENTS

Serves 4

1 onion, chopped

75g/3oz/6 tbsp unsalted butter

8 field mushrooms

15g/½oz/¼ cup dried ceps, bay boletus or saffron milk-caps, soaked in warm water for 20 minutes

1 garlic clove, crushed

75g/3oz/¾ cup fresh breadcrumbs

1 egg

75ml/5 tbsp chopped fresh parsley

15ml/1 tbsp chopped fresh thyme

salt and ground black pepper

115g/4oz prosciutto di Parma or San Daniele, thinly sliced

fresh parsley, to garnish

1 Preheat the oven to 190°C/375°F/Gas 5. Fry the onion gently in half the butter for 6–8 minutes until soft but not coloured. Meanwhile, break off the stems of the field mushrooms, setting the caps aside. Drain the dried mushrooms and chop these and the stems of the field mushrooms finely. Add to the onion together with the garlic and cook for a further 2–3 minutes.

2 Transfer the mixture to a bowl, add the breadcrumbs, egg, herbs and seasoning. Melt the remaining butter in a small pan and generously brush over the mushroom caps. Arrange the mushrooms on a baking sheet and spoon in the filling. Bake in the oven for 20–25 minutes until they are well browned.

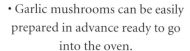

3 Top each mushroom with a slice of prosciutto, garnish with parsley and serve.

COOK'S TIP

• Garlic mushrooms can be easily prepared in advance ready to go into the oven.

• Fresh breadcrumbs can be made and then frozen. They can be taken from the freezer as they are required and do not need to be defrosted first.

Chicken with Lemon and Garlic

Extremely easy to cook and delicious to eat, serve this succulent tapas dish with home-made aioli if you like.

INGREDIENTS

Serves 4

225g/8oz skinless chicken breast fillets

30ml/2 tbsp olive oil

1 shallot, finely chopped

4 garlic cloves, finely chopped

5ml/1tsp paprika

juice of 1 lemon

30ml/2 tbsp chopped fresh parsley

salt and ground black pepper

flat leaf parsley, to garnish

lemon wedges, to serve

1 Sandwich the chicken breast fillets between two sheets of clear film or greaseproof paper. Bat out with a rolling pin or meat mallet until the fillets are about 5mm/¼ in thick.

2 Cut the chicken into strips about 1cm/½ in wide. Heat the oil in a large frying pan. Stir-fry the chicken strips with the shallot, garlic and paprika over a high heat for about 3 minutes until lightly browned and cooked through. Add the lemon juice and parsley with salt and pepper to taste. Serve with lemon wedges, garnished with flat leaf parsley.

Wilted Spinach and Bacon Salad

The hot dressing in this salad wilts the spinach and provides a taste sensation.

INGREDIENTS

Serves 6

450g/1lb fresh young spinach leaves

225g/8oz streaky bacon rashers

25ml/1½ tbsp vegetable oil

60ml/4 tbsp red wine vinegar

60ml/4 tbsp water

20ml/4 tsp caster sugar

5ml/1 tsp dry mustard

8 spring onions, thinly sliced

6 radishes, thinly sliced

2 hard-boiled eggs, coarsely grated

salt and ground black pepper

1 Pull any coarse stalks from the spinach leaves and rinse well. Put the leaves in a large salad bowl.

2 Fry the bacon rashers in the oil until crisp and brown. Remove with tongs and drain on paper towels. Reserve the cooking fat in the pan. Chop the bacon and set aside until needed.

3 Combine the vinegar, water, sugar, mustard, and salt and ground black pepper in a bowl and stir until smoothly blended. Add to the fat in the frying pan and stir to mix. Bring the dressing to the boil, stirring.

4 Pour the hot dressing evenly over the spinach leaves. Scatter the bacon, spring onions, radishes and eggs over, and toss, then serve.

Melon and Parma Ham Salad

Sections of cool fragrant melon wrapped with slices of air-dried ham make a delicious salad starter. If strawberries are in season, serve with a savoury-sweet strawberry salsa and watch it disappear.

Serves 4

1 large melon, cantaloupe, charentais
   or galia

175g/6oz Parma or Serrano ham,
   thinly sliced

For the salsa

225g/8oz/2 cups strawberries

5ml/1 tsp caster sugar

30ml/2 tbsp groundnut or sunflower oil

15ml/1 tbsp orange juice

2.5ml/½ tsp finely grated orange rind

2.5ml/½ tsp finely grated fresh
   root ginger

salt and ground black pepper

1 Halve the melon and scoop the seeds out with a spoon. Cut the rind away with a paring knife, then slice the melon thickly. Chill until ready to serve.

2 To make the salsa, hull the strawberries and cut them into large dice. Place in a small mixing bowl with the sugar and crush lightly to release the juices. Add the oil, orange juice, rind and ginger. Season with salt and plenty of ground black pepper.

3 Arrange the melon on a serving plate, lay the ham over the top and serve with a bowl of salsa, handed round separately.

Caesar Salad

This is a well-known and much enjoyed salad, even though its origins are a mystery. Be sure to use cos lettuce and add the very soft eggs at the last minute.

INGREDIENTS

Serves 6

175ml/6fl oz/³⁄₄ cup salad oil, preferably olive oil

115g/4oz French or Italian bread, cut in 2.5cm/1in cubes

1 large garlic clove, crushed with the flat side of a knife

1 cos lettuce

2 eggs, boiled for 1 minute

120ml/4fl oz/¹⁄₂ cup lemon juice

50g/2oz/²⁄₃ cup freshly grated Parmesan cheese

6 anchovy fillets, drained and finely chopped (optional)

salt and ground black pepper

1 Heat 50ml/2fl oz/¹⁄₄ cup of the oil in a large frying pan. Add the bread cubes and garlic. Fry, stirring and turning constantly, until the cubes are golden brown all over. Drain on kitchen paper. Discard the garlic.

2 Tear large lettuce leaves into smaller pieces. Then put all the lettuce in a bowl.

3 Add the remaining oil to the lettuce and season with salt and plenty of ground black pepper. Toss well to coat the leaves.

4 Break the eggs on top. Sprinkle with the lemon juice. Toss well again to combine.

5 Add the Parmesan cheese and anchovies, if using. Toss gently to mix.

6 Scatter the fried bread cubes on top and serve immediately.

COOK'S TIP

To make a tangier dressing mix 30ml/2 tbsp white wine vinegar, 15ml/1 tbsp Worcestershire sauce, 2.5ml/¹⁄₂ tsp mustard powder, 5ml/1 tsp sugar, salt and pepper in a screw-top jar, then add the oil and shake well.

Salade Niçoise

Made with the freshest ingredients, this classic Provençal salad makes a simple yet unbeatable summer dish. Serve with country-style bread and chilled white wine for a substantial starter.

Serves 4–6

115g/4oz French beans

1 tuna steak, about 175g/6oz

olive oil, for brushing

115g/4oz mixed salad leaves

½ small cucumber, thinly sliced

4 ripe tomatoes, quartered

50g/2oz can anchovies, drained and
    halved lengthways

4 hard-boiled eggs, quartered

½ bunch radishes, trimmed

50g/2oz/½ cup small black olives

salt and ground black pepper

flat leaf parsley, to garnish

For the dressing

90ml/6 tbsp virgin olive oil

2 garlic cloves, crushed

15ml/1 tbsp white wine vinegar

salt and ground black pepper

1 Whisk together the oil, garlic and vinegar then season to taste with salt and pepper.

2 Preheat the grill. Brush the tuna steak with olive oil and season with salt and black pepper. Grill for 3–4 minutes on each side until cooked through. Set aside and leave to cool.

3 Trim and halve the French beans. Cook them in a pan of boiling water for 2 minutes until only just tender, then drain, refresh and leave to cool.

4 Mix together the salad leaves, sliced cucumber, tomatoes and French beans in a large, shallow bowl. Flake the tuna steak with your fingers or two forks.

5 Scatter the tuna, anchovies, eggs, radishes and olives over the salad. Pour over the dressing and toss together lightly. Serve garnished with parsley.

Mushroom Salad with Parma Ham

Pancake ribbons create a lovely light texture to this starter. Use whatever edible wild mushrooms you can find, or substitute interesting cultivated varieties if you need to.

INGREDIENTS

Serves 4

40g/1½ oz/3 tbsp unsalted butter

450g/1lb assorted wild and cultivated
    mushrooms such as chanterelles, ceps,
    bay boletus, Caesar's mushrooms,
    oyster, field and Paris mushrooms,
    trimmed and sliced

60ml/4 tbsp Madeira or sherry

juice of ½ lemon

½ oak leaf lettuce

½ frisée lettuce

30ml/2 tbsp walnut oil

salt and ground black pepper

For the pancake and ham ribbons

25g/1oz/3 tbsp plain flour

75ml/5 tbsp milk

1 egg

60ml/4 tbsp freshly grated
    Parmesan cheese

60ml/4 tbsp chopped fresh herbs such as
    parsley, thyme, marjoram or chives

salt and pepper

butter, for frying

175g/6oz Parma ham, thickly sliced

1 To make the pancakes, blend the flour and the milk. Beat in the egg, cheese, herbs and some seasoning. Heat the butter in a frying pan and pour enough of the mixture to coat the base. When the batter has set, turn the pancake over and cook until firm.

2 Turn out and cool. Roll up the pancake and slice to make 1cm/½in ribbons. Cook the remaining batter the same way and cut the ham into similar sized ribbons. Toss with the pancake ribbons. Set aside.

3 Gently soften the mushrooms in the butter for 6–8 minutes until the moisture has evaporated. Add the Madeira or sherry and lemon juice; season.

4 Toss the salad leaves in the oil and arrange on four plates. Place the Parma ham and pancake ribbons in the centre, spoon on the mushrooms and serve.

Avocado and Smoked Fish Salad

Avocado and smoked fish make a good combination, and flavoured with herbs and spices, create a delectable and elegant starter.

INGREDIENTS

Serves 4

15g/½oz/1 tbsp butter or margarine
½ onion, finely sliced
5ml/1 tsp mustard seeds
225g/8oz smoked mackerel, flaked
30ml/2 tbsp fresh chopped coriander
2 firm tomatoes, peeled and chopped
15ml/1 tbsp lemon juice

For the salad
2 avocados
½ cucumber
15ml/1 tbsp lemon juice
2 firm tomatoes
1 green chilli
salt and ground black pepper

1 Melt the butter or margarine in a frying pan, add the onion and mustard seeds and fry for about 5 minutes until the onion is soft but not browned.

2 Add the fish, chopped coriander, tomatoes and lemon juice and cook over a low heat for about 2–3 minutes. Remove from the heat and leave to cool.

COOK'S TIP
∽

Smoked mackerel has a distinctive flavour, but smoked haddock or cod can also be used in this salad, or a mixture of mackerel and haddock. For a speedy salad, canned tuna makes a convenient substitute.

3 To make the salad, slice the avocados and cucumber thinly. Place together in a bowl and sprinkle with the lemon juice to prevent discoloration.

4 Slice the tomatoes and seed and finely chop the chilli.

5 Place the fish mixture in the centre of a serving plate.

6 Arrange the avocado slices, cucumber and tomatoes decoratively around the outside of the fish. Alternatively, spoon a quarter of the fish mixture on to each of four serving plates and divide the avocados, cucumber and tomatoes equally among them. Then sprinkle with the chopped chilli and a little salt and ground black pepper, and serve.

Vegetarian

The freshest of vegetables cooked with the lightest of touches can be unforgettable. Tomato and Courgette Timbales are undeniably elegant, a classic Risotto Alla Milanese is perfect for a winter's day and there's nothing like a simple Roasted Tomato and Mozzarella Salad for *al fresco* dining.

Asparagus with Raspberry Dressing

Asparagus and raspberries complement each other. The sauce gives this starter a real zing.

INGREDIENTS

Serves 4

675g/1½lb thin asparagus spears
30ml/2 tbsp raspberry vinegar
2.5ml/½ tsp salt
5ml/1 tsp Dijon mustard
25ml/1½ tbsp sunflower oil
30ml/2 tbsp soured cream or
    natural yogurt
ground white pepper
175g/6oz/1 cup fresh raspberries

1 Fill a large wide frying pan or wok with water 10cm/4in deep and bring to the boil.

2 Trim the tough ends of the asparagus spears. If desired, remove the "scales" using a vegetable peeler.

3 Tie the asparagus spears into two bundles. Lower the bundles into the boiling water and cook until just tender, about 2 minutes.

4 Using a fish slice, carefully remove the asparagus bundles from the frying pan or wok and immerse in cold water to stop the cooking. Drain then untie the bundles. Pat dry with kitchen paper. Chill the asparagus in the fridge for at least 1 hour.

5 Combine the vinegar and salt in a bowl and stir with a fork until dissolved. Stir in the mustard. Gradually stir in the oil until it is blended. Add the soured cream or yogurt and pepper to taste.

6 To serve, place the asparagus on individual plates and drizzle the dressing across the middle of the spears. Garnish with the fresh raspberries.

Aubergine and Smoked Mozzarella Rolls

Slices of grilled aubergine are stuffed with smoked mozzarella, tomato and fresh basil to make an attractive hors-d'oeuvre. The rolls are also good barbecued.

INGREDIENTS

Serves 4

1 large aubergine

45ml/3 tbsp olive oil, plus extra for
  drizzling (optional)

165g/5½ oz smoked mozzarella cheese,
  cut into 8 slices

2 plum tomatoes, each cut into
  4 even-size slices

8 large basil leaves

balsamic vinegar, for drizzling (optional)

salt and ground black pepper

1 Cut the aubergine lengthways into 10 thin slices and discard the two outermost slices. Sprinkle the slices with salt and set them aside for 20 minutes. Rinse, then pat dry with kitchen paper.

2 Preheat the grill and line the rack with foil. Place the dried aubergine slices on the grill rack and brush liberally with oil. Grill for 8–10 minutes until tender and golden, turning once.

3 Remove the aubergine slices from the grill, then place a slice of mozzarella and tomato and a basil leaf in the centre of each aubergine slice, and season to taste. Fold the aubergine over the filling and cook seam-side down under the grill until heated through and the mozzarella begins to melt. Serve drizzled with olive oil and a little balsamic vinegar, if using.

Tomato and Courgette Timbales

Timbales are baked savoury custards typical of the South of France, and mainly made with light vegetables. This combination is delicious as a starter. It can be served warm or cool. Try other combinations if you like and choose different herbs as well.

INGREDIENTS

Serves 4

a little butter

2 courgettes, about 175g/6oz

2 firm, ripe vine tomatoes, sliced

2 eggs plus 2 egg yolks

45ml/3 tbsp double cream

15ml/1 tbsp fresh tomato sauce or passata

10ml/2 tsp chopped fresh basil or oregano or 5ml/1 tsp dried

salt and ground black pepper

salad leaves, to serve

1 Preheat the oven to 180°C/350°F/Gas 4. Lightly butter four large ramekins. Top and tail the courgettes then cut them into thin slices. Put them into a steamer and steam over boiling water for 4–5 minutes. Drain well in a colander then layer the courgettes in the ramekins alternating with the sliced tomatoes.

2 Whisk together the eggs, cream, tomato sauce or passata, herbs and seasoning. Pour the egg mixture into the ramekins. Place them in a roasting tin and half fill with hot water. Bake the ramekins for 20–30 minutes until the custard is just firm.

3 Cool slightly then run a knife round the rims and carefully turn out on to small plates. Serve with salad leaves.

COOK'S TIP

Don't overcook the timbales or the texture of the savoury custard will become rubbery.

Poached Eggs Florentine

The term "à la Florentine" means "in the style of Florence" and refers to dishes cooked with spinach and topped with mornay sauce. Here is a subtly spiced, elegant starter.

INGREDIENTS

Serves 4

675g/1½ lb spinach, washed and drained

25g/1oz/2 tbsp butter

60ml/4 tbsp double cream

pinch of freshly grated nutmeg

salt and ground black pepper

For the topping

25g/1oz/2 tbsp butter

25g/1oz/¼ cup plain flour

300ml/½ pint/1¼ cups hot milk

pinch of ground mace

115g/4oz Gruyère cheese, grated

4 eggs

15ml/1 tbsp freshly grated
   Parmesan cheese, plus shavings to serve

1 Place the spinach in a large pan with very little water. Cook for 3–4 minutes or until tender, then drain and chop finely. Return the spinach to the pan, add the butter, cream, nutmeg and seasoning and heat through. Place in the base of one large or four small gratin dishes.

2 To make the topping, heat the butter in a small pan, add the flour and cook for 1 minute to a paste. Gradually blend in the hot milk, beating well as it thickens to break up any lumps.

3 Cook for 1–2 minutes stirring. Remove from the heat and stir in the mace and three-quarters of the Gruyère cheese.

4 Preheat the oven to 200°C/400°F/Gas 6. Poach the eggs in lightly salted water for 3–4 minutes. Make hollows in the spinach with the back of a spoon, and place a poached egg in each one. Cover with the cheese sauce and sprinkle with the remaining Gruyère and Parmesan. Bake for 10 minutes or until golden. Serve at once with Parmesan shavings.

Risotto with Four Cheeses

This is a very rich dish. Serve it for a special dinner-party first course, with a light, dry sparkling white wine to accompany it.

INGREDIENTS

Serves 4–6

40g/1½oz/3 tbsp butter

1 small onion, finely chopped

1.2 litres/2 pints/5 cups vegetable stock, preferably home-made

350g/12oz/1¾ cups risotto rice

200ml/7fl oz/scant 1 cup dry white wine

50g/2oz/½ cup grated Gruyère cheese

50g/2oz/½ cup diced taleggio cheese

50g/2oz/½ cup diced Gorgonzola cheese

50g/2oz/⅔ cup freshly grated Parmesan cheese

salt and ground black pepper

chopped fresh flat leaf parsley, to garnish

1 Melt the butter in a large, heavy-based saucepan or deep frying pan and fry the onion over a gentle heat for about 4–5 minutes, stirring frequently, until softened and lightly browned. Pour the stock into a separate pan and heat it to simmering point.

2 Add the rice to the onion mixture, stir until the grains start to swell and burst, then add the wine. Stir until it stops sizzling and most of it has been absorbed by the rice, then pour in a little of the hot stock. Add salt and ground black pepper to taste. Stir the rice over a low heat until the stock has been absorbed.

3 Gradually add the remaining stock, a little at a time, allowing the rice to absorb the liquid before adding more, and stirring constantly. After about 20–25 minutes the rice will be *al dente* and the risotto will have a creamy consistency.

4 Turn off the heat under the pan, then add the Gruyère, taleggio, the Gorgonzola and 30ml/2 tbsp of the Parmesan. Stir gently until the cheeses have melted, then taste for seasoning. Spoon into a serving bowl and garnish with parsley. Serve the remaining Parmesan separately.

Risotto Alla Milanese

This classic risotto can be served as an accompaniment to a main dish, but it also makes a delicious first course in its own right.

INGREDIENTS

Serves 5–6

about 1.2 litres/2 pints/5 cups
   vegetable stock
good pinch of saffron strands
75g/3oz/6 tbsp butter
1 onion, finely chopped
275g/10oz/1½ cups risotto rice
75g/3oz/1 cup freshly grated
   Parmesan cheese
salt and ground black pepper

3 Add the rice. Stir until the grains start to swell and burst, then add a few ladlefuls of the stock, with the saffron liquid and salt and pepper to taste. Stir over a low heat until the stock has been absorbed. Add the remaining stock, a few ladlefuls at a time, allowing the rice to absorb all the liquid before adding more, and stirring constantly. After about 20–25 minutes, the rice should be just tender and the risotto golden yellow, moist and creamy.

4 Gently stir in about two-thirds of the grated Parmesan and the remaining butter. Heat through until the butter has melted, then taste for seasoning. Transfer the risotto to a warmed serving bowl or platter and serve hot, with the remaining grated Parmesan served separately.

1 Bring the stock to the boil, then reduce to a low simmer. Ladle a little stock into a small bowl. Add the saffron strands and leave to infuse.

2 Melt 50g/2oz/4 tbsp of the butter in a large saucepan until foaming. Add the onion and cook gently for about 3 minutes, stirring frequently, until softened but not browned at all.

Pears and Stilton

Stilton is the classic British blue cheese, but you could use blue Cheshire instead, or even a non-British cheese such as Gorgonzola.

INGREDIENTS

Serves 4

4 ripe pears, lightly chilled

75g/3oz blue Stilton

50g/2oz curd cheese

ground black pepper

watercress sprigs, to garnish

For the dressing

45ml/3 tbsp light olive oil

15ml/1 tbsp lemon juice

10ml/2 tsp toasted poppy seeds

salt and ground black pepper

1 First make the dressing, place the olive oil and lemon juice, poppy seeds and seasoning in a screw-top jar and then shake together until emulsified.

2 Cut the pears in half lengthways, then scoop out the cores and cut away the calyx from the rounded end.

3 Beat together the Stilton, curd cheese and a little pepper. Divide this mixture among the cavities in the pears.

4 Shake the dressing to mix it again, then spoon it over the pears. Serve garnished with some watercress sprigs.

COOK'S TIP

Comice pears are a good choice for this dish, being very juicy and aromatic. For a dramatic colour contrast, select the excellent sweet and juicy Red Williams.

Fried Rice Balls Stuffed with Mozzarella

These deep-fried balls of risotto go by the name of Suppli al Telefono in their native Italy. Stuffed with mozzarella cheese, they are very popular snacks, which is hardly surprising as they are quite delicious. They make a wonderful start to any meal.

INGREDIENTS

Serves 4

1 quantity Risotto alla Milanese,
    made without the saffron
    (see page 113)
3 eggs
breadcrumbs and plain flour, to coat
115g/4oz/⅔ cup mozzarella cheese, cut
    into small cubes
oil, for deep-frying
dressed curly endive and cherry tomatoes,
    to serve

1 Put the risotto in a bowl and allow it to cool completely. Beat two of the eggs, and stir them into the cooled risotto until well mixed.

2 Use your hands to form the rice mixture into balls the size of a large egg. If the mixture is too moist to hold its shape well, stir in a few spoonfuls of breadcrumbs. Poke a hole in the centre of each ball with your finger, then fill it with small cubes of mozzarella, and close the hole over again with the rice mixture.

3 Heat the oil for deep-frying until a small piece of bread sizzles as soon as it is dropped in.

4 Spread some flour on a plate. Beat the remaining egg in a shallow bowl. Sprinkle another plate with breadcrumbs. Roll the balls in the flour, then in the egg, and finally in the breadcrumbs.

5 Fry the rice balls, a few at a time, in the hot oil until golden and crisp. Drain on kitchen paper while the remaining balls are being fried and keep warm. Serve at once, with a simple salad of dressed curly endive leaves and cherry tomatoes.

COOK'S TIP

These provide the perfect solution as to what to do with leftover risotto, as they are best made with a cold mixture, cooked the day before.

Courgette Fritters with Chilli Jam

Chilli jam is hot, sweet and sticky – rather like a thick chutney. It adds a delicious piquancy to these light courgette fritters which are always a popular dish.

INGREDIENTS

Makes 12 Fritters

450g/1lb/3½ cups coarsely grated courgettes
50g/2oz/⅔ cup freshly grated Parmesan cheese
2 eggs, beaten
60ml/4 tbsp plain flour
vegetable oil, for frying
salt and ground black pepper

For the chilli jam

75ml/5 tbsp olive oil
4 large onions, diced
4 garlic cloves, chopped
1–2 green chillies, seeded and sliced
30ml/2 tbsp dark brown soft sugar

1 First make the chilli jam. Heat the oil in a frying pan until hot, then add the onions and the garlic. Reduce the heat to low, then cook for 20 minutes, stirring frequently, until the onions are very soft.

> #### COOK'S TIP
>
> Stored in an airtight jar in the fridge, the chilli jam will keep for up to 1 week

2 Leave the onion mixture to cool, then transfer to a food processor or blender. Add the chillies and sugar and blend until smooth, then return the mixture to the saucepan. Cook for a further 10 minutes, stirring frequently, until the liquid evaporates and the mixture has the consistency of jam. Cool slightly.

3 To make the fritters, squeeze the courgettes in a dish towel to remove any excess liquid, then combine with the Parmesan, eggs, flour and salt and pepper.

4 Heat enough oil to cover the base of a large frying pan. Add 30ml/2 tbsp of the mixture for each fritter and cook three fritters at a time. Cook for 2–3 minutes on each side until golden, then keep warm while you cook the rest of the fritters. Drain on kitchen paper and serve warm with a spoonful of the chilli jam.

Goat's Cheese Salad

Goat's cheese has a strong, tangy flavour so choose robust salad leaves to accompany it.

INGREDIENTS

Serves 4

30ml/2 tbsp olive oil

4 slices of French bread, 1cm/½ in thick

8 cups mixed salad leaves, such as curly endive, radicchio and red oak leaf, torn in small pieces

4 firm goat's cheese rounds, about 50g/2oz each, rind removed

1 yellow or red pepper, seeded and finely diced

1 small red onion, thinly sliced

45ml/3 tbsp chopped fresh parsley

30ml/2 tbsp snipped fresh chives

For the dressing

30ml/2 tbsp white wine vinegar

1.5ml/¼ tsp salt

5ml/1 tsp wholegrain mustard

75ml/5 tbsp olive oil

ground black pepper

1 For the dressing, mix the vinegar and salt with a fork until dissolved. Stir in the mustard. Gradually stir in the olive oil until blended. Season with pepper and set aside until needed.

2 Preheat the grill. Heat the oil in a skillet. When hot, add the bread slices and fry until golden, about 1 minute. Turn and cook on the other side, about 30 seconds more. Drain on kitchen paper and set aside.

3 Place the salad leaves in a bowl. Add 45ml/3 tbsp of the dressing and toss to coat well. Divide the dressed leaves among four salad plates.

4 Preheat the grill. Place the goat's cheeses, cut sides up, on a baking sheet and grill until bubbling and golden, about 1–2 minutes.

5 Set a goat's cheese on each slice of bread and place in the centre of each plate. Scatter the diced pepper, red onion, parsley and chives over the salad. Drizzle with the remaining dressing and serve.

Black Pasta with Ricotta

This is designer pasta – which is coloured with squid ink – at its most dramatic, the kind of dish you are most likely to see at a fashionable Italian restaurant. Serve it for a smart dinner-party first course – it will create a great talking point.

INGREDIENTS

Serves 4

300g/11oz dried black pasta

60ml/4 tbsp ricotta cheese, as fresh
   as possible

60ml/4 tbsp extra virgin olive oil

1 small fresh red chilli, seeded and
   finely chopped

small handful of fresh basil leaves

salt and ground black pepper

1 Cook the black pasta in salted boiling water according to the instructions on the packet. Meanwhile, put the ricotta in a bowl, add salt and pepper to taste and use a little of the hot water from the pasta pan to mix it to a smooth, creamy consistency. Taste for seasoning.

2 Drain the pasta. Heat the oil gently in the clean pan and add the pasta with the chilli and salt and pepper to taste. Toss quickly over a high heat to combine.

3 Divide the pasta equally among four warmed bowls, then top with the ricotta cheese. Sprinkle with the basil leaves and serve immediately. Each diner tosses their own portion of pasta and cheese.

COOK'S TIP

If you prefer, use green spinach-flavoured pasta or red tomato-flavoured pasta in place of the black pasta.

Paglia e Fieno with Walnuts and Gorgonzola

Cheese and nuts are popular ingredients for pasta sauces. The combination is very rich, so reserve this dish for a dinner-party starter. The contrasting colours make this dish look particularly attractive. It needs no accompaniment other than wine – a dry white would be good.

INGREDIENTS

Serves 4

275g/10oz dried paglia e fieno

25g/1oz/2 tbsp butter

5ml/1 tsp finely chopped fresh sage, or
   2.5ml/½ tsp dried, plus fresh sage
   leaves, to garnish (optional)

115g/4oz/1 cup Gorgonzola cheese, diced

45ml/3 tbsp mascarpone cheese

75ml/5 tbsp milk

50g/2oz/½ cup walnut halves, ground

30ml/2 tbsp freshly grated
   Parmesan cheese

ground black pepper

1 Cook the pasta in a large saucepan of salted boiling water, according to the instructions on the packet. Meanwhile, melt the butter in a large skillet or saucepan over a low heat, add the sage and stir it around. Sprinkle in the diced Gorgonzola and then add the mascarpone. Stir the ingredients with a wooden spoon until the cheeses start to melt. Pour in the milk and keep stirring.

2 Sprinkle in the walnuts and grated Parmesan and add plenty of black pepper. Continue to stir over a low heat until the mixture forms a creamy sauce. Do not allow it to boil or the nuts will taste bitter, and do not cook the sauce for longer than a few minutes or the nuts will begin to discolour it.

3 Drain the pasta, tip it into a warmed bowl, then add the sauce and toss well. Serve immediately, with more black pepper ground on top. Garnish with sage leaves, if using.

Pear and Parmesan Salad

This is a good starter when pears are at their seasonal best. Try Packhams or Comice when plentiful, drizzled with a poppy-seed dressing and topped with shavings of Parmesan.

INGREDIENTS

Serves 4

4 just-ripe dessert pears

50g/2oz piece Parmesan cheese

watercress, to garnish

water biscuits or rye bread, to
    serve (optional)

For the dressing

30ml/2 tbsp extra virgin olive oil

15ml/1 tbsp sunflower oil

30ml/2 tbsp cider vinegar or white
    wine vinegar

2.5ml/½ tsp soft light brown sugar

good pinch of dried thyme

15ml/1 tbsp poppy seeds

salt and ground black pepper

1 Cut the pears in quarters and remove the cores. Cut each pear quarter in half lengthways and arrange them on four small serving plates. Peel the pears if you wish, though they look more attractive unpeeled.

2 Make the dressing. Mix the oils, vinegar, sugar, thyme and seasoning in a jug. Whisk well, then tip in the poppy seeds. Trickle the dressing over the pears. Garnish with watercress and shave Parmesan over the top. Serve with water biscuits or thinly sliced rye bread, if you like.

COOK'S TIP

Blue cheeses and pears also have a natural affinity Stilton, dolcelatte, Gorgonzola or Danish blue are good substitutes. Allow about 200g/7oz and cut into wedges or cubes. This makes a slightly more substantial first course, so follow with a light dish.

Panzanella Salad

If sliced juicy tomatoes layered with day-old bread sounds strange for a salad, don't be deceived – it's quite delicious. A popular Italian salad, this dish is ideal for serving as a starter. Use full-flavoured tomatoes for the best result.

INGREDIENTS

Serves 4–6

4 thick slices day-old bread, either white, brown or rye

1 small red onion, thinly sliced

450g/1lb ripe tomatoes, thinly sliced

115g/4oz mozzarella cheese, thinly sliced

5ml/1 tbsp fresh basil, shredded, or fresh marjoram

120ml/4fl oz/½ cup extra virgin olive oil

45ml/3 tbsp balsamic vinegar

juice or 1 small lemon

salt and ground black pepper

stoned and sliced black olives or salted capers, to garnish

1 Dip the bread briefly in cold water, then carefully squeeze out the excess water. Arrange the bread in the base of a shallow salad bowl.

2 Soak the onion slices in cold water for about 10 minutes while you prepare the other ingredients. Drain and reserve.

3 Layer the tomatoes, cheese, onion, basil or marjoram, seasoning well in between each layer. Sprinkle with oil, vinegar and lemon juice.

4 Top with the olives or capers, cover with clear film and chill in the fridge for at least 2 hours or overnight, if possible.

Asparagus and Orange Salad

A simple dressing of olive oil and vinegar mingles with the orange and tomato flavours with great results.

INGREDIENTS

Serves 4

225g/8oz asparagus, trimmed and cut into
    5cm/2in pieces

2 large oranges

2 well-flavoured ripe tomatoes, cut
    into eighths

50g/2oz romaine lettuce leaves, shredded

30ml/2 tbsp extra virgin olive oil

2.5ml/½ tsp sherry vinegar

salt and ground black pepper

1 Cook the asparagus in boiling, salted water for 3–4 minutes, until just tender. Drain and refresh under cold water. Set aside.

2 Grate the rind from half an orange and reserve. Peel all the oranges and cut into segments, leaving the membrane behind. Squeeze out the juice from the membrane and reserve the juice.

3 Put the asparagus, orange segments, tomatoes and lettuce into a salad bowl. Mix together the oil and vinegar and add 15ml/1 tbsp of the reserved orange juice and 5ml/1 tsp of the rind. Season with salt and plenty of ground black pepper. Just before serving, pour the dressing over the salad and mix gently to coat.

Tricolour Salad

A popular salad, this dish depends for its success on the quality of its ingredients. Mozzarella di bufala is the best cheese to serve uncooked. Whole ripe plum tomatoes give up their juice to blend with extra virgin olive oil for a natural dressing.

INGREDIENTS

Serves 2–3

150g/5oz mozzarella di bufala cheese,
   thinly sliced

4 large plum tomatoes, sliced

1 large avocado

about 12 basil leaves or a small handful of
   flat leaf parsley leaves

45–60ml/3–4 tbsp extra virgin olive oil

ground black pepper

ciabatta and sea salt flakes, to serve

1 Arrange the sliced mozzarella cheese and tomatoes randomly on two salad plates. Crush over a few good pinches of sea salt flakes. This will help to draw out some of the juices from the plum tomatoes. Set aside in a cool place and leave to marinate for about 30 minutes.

2 Just before serving, cut the avocado in half using a large sharp knife and twist the halves to separate. Lift out the stone and remove the peel.

3 Carefully slice the avocado flesh crossways into half moons, or cut it into large chunks if that is easier.

4 Place the avocado on the salad, then sprinkle with the basil or parsley. Drizzle over the olive oil, add a little more salt if liked and some black pepper. Serve at room temperature, with chunks of crusty Italian ciabatta for mopping up the dressing.

Roasted Tomato and Mozzarella Salad

Roasting the tomatoes brings out their sweetness and adds a new dimension to this salad. Make the basil oil just before serving to retain its fresh flavour and vivid colour.

INGREDIENTS

Serves 4

6 large plum tomatoes

olive oil, for brushing

2 fresh mozzarella cheese balls, cut into
   8–12 slices

salt and ground black pepper

basil leaves, to garnish

For the basil oil

25 basil leaves

60ml/4 tbsp extra virgin olive oil

1 garlic clove, crushed

1 Preheat the oven to 200°C/
400°F/Gas 6 and oil a baking tray. Cut the tomatoes in half lengthways and remove the seeds. Place the halves skin-side down on the baking tray and roast for 20 minutes or until the tomatoes are very tender but still retain their shape.

2 Meanwhile, make the basil oil. Place the basil leaves, olive oil and garlic in a food processor or blender and process until smooth. You will need to scrape down the sides once or twice to ensure the mixture is processed properly. Transfer to a bowl and chill until required.

3 For each serving, place the tomato halves on top of 2 or 3 slices of mozzarella and drizzle over the oil. Season well. Garnish with basil leaves and serve at once.

Mixed Herb Salad with Toasted Mixed Seeds

This simple salad is the perfect antidote to a rich, heavy meal as it contains fresh herbs that can ease the digestion. Balsamic vinegar adds a rich, sweet taste to the dressing, but red or white wine vinegar could be used instead.

INGREDIENTS

Serves 4

90g/3½oz/4 cups mixed salad leaves

50g/2oz/2 cups mixed salad herbs, such as
   coriander, parsley, basil, chervil
   and rocket

25g/1oz/3 tbsp pumpkin seeds

25g/1oz/3 tbsp sunflower seeds

For the dressing

60ml/4 tbsp extra virgin olive oil

15ml/1 tbsp balsamic vinegar

2.5ml/½ tsp Dijon mustard

salt and ground black pepper

1 To make the dressing, combine the ingredients in a bowl or screw-top jar. Mix with a small whisk or fork, or shake well, until completely combined.

2 Put the salad leaves and herb leaves in a large bowl. Toss with your fingers to mix together.

3 Toast the pumpkin and sunflower seeds in a dry frying pan over a medium heat for about 2 minutes until golden, tossing frequently to prevent them burning. Allow the seeds to cool slightly before sprinkling them over the salad.

4 Pour the dressing over the salad and toss with your hands until the leaves are well coated, then serve.

Index

A
almond soup, chilled 20
asparagus and egg
    terrine 51
asparagus and
    langoustine,
    marinated 77
asparagus and orange
    salad 122
asparagus with raspberry
    dressing 108
asparagus with salt-
    cured ham,
    grilled 94
aubergines
    aubergine and
        smoked mozzarella
        rolls 109
    Greek aubergine and
        spinach pie 68–9
avocado and smoked
    fish salad 105
avocado, prawn and egg
    mousses 42
avocado salsa with
    gazpacho 27

B
basil and clam soup 32
basil and melon soup 19
beans
    cannellini bean and
        rosemary
        bruschetta 73
    clams with chilli and
        yellow bean
        sauce 78
    salade Niçoise 103
black pasta with
    ricotta 118–19
brandade of salt cod 45
bread
    Caesar salad 102
    cannellini bean and
        rosemary
        bruschetta 73
    griddled tomatoes on
        soda bread 65
    panzanella salad 121
breaded sole batons
    91
broccoli soup with
    garlic toast 18

C
Caesar salad 102
cannellini bean and
    rosemary bruschetta 73
cheese

aubergine and
    mozzarella
    rolls 109
black pasta with
    ricotta 118–19
crab and ricotta
    tartlets 61
creamy courgette and
    Dolcelatte soup 22
fried rice balls
    stuffed with
    mozzarella 115
goat's cheese
    salad 117
marinated feta
cheese with
    capers 72
paglia e fieno with
    walnuts and
    Gorgonzola 118–19
Parmesan fish
goujons 92
pear and Parmesan
    salad 120
pears and Stilton
    114
risotto alla
    Milanese 113
risotto with four
    cheeses 112
roasted tomato and
    mozzarella
    salad 124–5
tricolour salad 123
twice-baked Gruyère
    cheese and potato
    soufflé 56
wild mushroom and
    fontina tarts 63
cherry soup, Hungarian
    sour 23
chicken and pork
    terrine 55
chicken bitki 96
chicken liver pâté 40
chicken with lemon and
    garlic 99
chilled almond soup 20
chilled prawn and
    cucumber soup 26
chilled tomato and
    sweet pepper soup 11
chilli
    clams with chilli and
        yellow bean
        sauce 78
    courgette fritters
        with chilli jam 116
clam and basil soup 32
clams with chilli and
    yellow bean sauce 78

consommé with
    agnolotti 34–5

courgette and Dolcelatte
    soup 22
courgette and tomato
    timbales 110
courgette fritters with
    chilli jam 116
crab and ricotta
    tartlets 61
crab cakes with tartare
    sauce 88–9
crab soufflés, hot 57
cucumber
    chilled prawn and
        cucumber soup 26
    cold cucumber and
        yogurt soup 10
    gazpacho with
        avocado salsa 27

D
deep-fried whitebait 93

E
eggs
    asparagus and egg
        terrine 51
    Caesar salad 102
    egg and salmon puff
        parcels 70
    poached eggs
        Florentine 111
    prawn and egg-knot
        soup 30
    prawn, egg and
        avocado mousses 42

quail's eggs in aspic
    with Parma ham 9

F
fish
    avocado and
        smoked fish
        salad 105
    brandade of salt
        cod 45
    breaded sole
        batons 91
    deep-fried
        whitebait 93
    egg and salmon puff
        parcels 70
    fish soup with
        rouille 33
    haddock and smoked
        salmon terrine 52–3
    monkfish
        packages 86
    Parmesan fish
        goujons 92
    potted salmon with
        lemon and dill 46
    salade Niçoise 103
    salmon cakes with
        butter sauce 90
    salmon rillettes 44
    sea trout
        mousse 43
    smoked haddock
        pâté 39
    smoked salmon and
        rice salad parcels 85
    smoked salmon
        pâté 38

three-colour fish
kebabs 87
five-spice rib-sticker 97
French onion and morel
soup 15
fresh tomato soup 17
fried rice balls stuffed
with mozzarella 115
fried squid 82–3
fruit
asparagus and orange
salad 122
asparagus with
raspberry
dressing 108
Hungarian sour
cherry soup 23
melon and basil
soup 19
melon and Parma
ham salad 101
pear and Parmesan
salad 120
pears and Stilton 114
watercress and
orange soup 25

G
garlic
garlic prawns in filo
tartlets 60
garlic toast with
broccoli soup 18
Spanish garlic
soup 14
stuffed garlic
mushrooms with
prosciutto 98
gazpacho with
avocado salsa 27
goat's cheese salad 117
Greek aubergine and
spinach pie 68–9
griddled tomatoes on
soda bread 65
grilled asparagus with
salt-cured ham 94
grilled scallops with
brown butter 82–3
grilled vegetable
terrine 48–9

H
haddock and smoked
salmon terrine
52–3
haddock pâté,
smoked 39
herbs
cannellini bean and
rosemary bruschetta 73
clam and basil
soup 32
herbed pâté pie 41

mixed herb salad
with toasted mixed
seeds 124–5
spotted salmon with
lemon and dill 46
tiger prawns with
mint, dill and
lime 62
hot and sour prawn
soup with lemon
grass 31
hot crab soufflés 57
hot-and-sour soup 28
Hungarian sour cherry
soup 23

L
langoustine and
asparagus,
marinated 77
leek and onion
tartlets 64
lemon grass
hot and sour prawn
soup with lemon
grass 31
hot and sour soup 28
mussels and clams
and lemon grass 79
lemons
chicken with lemon
and garlic 99
potted salmon with
lemon and dill 46
lime, mint and dill with
tiger prawns 62

M
Malayan prawn laska 29
marinated asparagus
and langoustine 77
marinated feta cheese
with capers 72
melon and basil soup 19
melon and Parma ham
salad 101
mixed herb salad with
toasted mixed
seeds 124–5
monkfish packages
86
mushrooms
chicken bitki 96
French onion and
morel soup 15
mushroom salad with
Parma ham 104
stuffed garlic
mushrooms with
prosciutto 98
tortellini chanterelle
broth 13
wild mushroom and
fontina tarts 63

wild mushroom
soup 16
mussels and clams with
lemon grass 79

N
nuts
chilled almond
soup 20
paglia e fieno with
walnuts and
Gorgonzola 118–19

O
onion and leek
tartlets 64
onion and morel soup,
French 15
orange and asparagus
salad 122
orange and watercress
soup 25

P
paella croquettes 84
panzanella salad 121
Parmesan fish goujons
92
pasta
black pasta with
ricotta 118–19
consommé with
agnolotti 34–5
paglia e fieno with
walnuts and
Gorgonzola 118–19
tortellini chanterelle
broth 13
pear and Parmesan

salad 120
pear and watercress
soup 12
pears and Stilton 114
peppers
chilled tomato and
sweet pepper
soup 11
gazpacho with
avocado salsa 27
roast pepper
terrine 50
scallop-stuffed roast
peppers with
pesto 81
poached eggs
Florentine 111
pork
chicken and pork
terrine 55
five-spice
rib-sticker 97
grilled asparagus
with salt-cured
ham 94
herbed liver pâté
pie 41
melon and Parma
ham salad 101
mushroom salad with
Parma ham 104
quail's eggs in aspic
with Parma ham 95
scallops wrapped in
Parma ham 80
stuffed garlic
mushrooms with
prosciutto 98
wilted spinach and

bacon salad 100
potatoes and Gruyère
cheese soufflé,
twice-baked 56
potted prawns 47
potted salmon with lemon
and dill 46
prawn and cucumber
soup, chilled 26
prawn and egg-knot
soup 30
prawn cocktail 76
prawn, egg and avocado
mousses 42
prawn laksa,
Malayan 29
prawn soup with lemon
grass, hot and sour 31
prawns in filo
tartlets 60
prawns, potted 47
prawns with mint, dill
and lime 62

Q
quail's eggs in aspic
with Parma ham 95

R
raspberry and asparagus
dressing 108
rice
fried rice balls
stuffed with
mozzarella 115
risotto alla
Milanese 113
risotto with four
cheeses 112
smoked salmon and
rice salad parcels 85
spinach and rice soup 21
roast pepper terrine 50
roasted tomato and
mozzarella
salad 124–5
rouille with fish
soup 33

S
salade Niçoise 103
salmon and egg puff
parcels 70
salmon and haddock
terrine 52–3
salmon and rice salad
parcels 85
salmon cakes with butter
sauce 90
salmon pâté, smoked
38
salmon rillettes 44
salmon with lemon and
dill, potted 46

sauces
crab cakes with tartare
sauce 88–9
salmon cakes with
butter sauce 90
scallop-stuffed roast
peppers with pesto
81
scallops with brown
butter, grilled 82–3
scallops wrapped in
Parma ham 80
sea trout mousse 43
shellfish
chilled prawn and
cucumber soup 26
clam and basil soup 32
clams with chilli and
yellow bean sauce 78
consommé with
agnolotti 34–5
crab and ricotta
tartlets 61
crab cakes with tartare
sauce 88–9
fried squid 82–3
garlic prawns in filo
tartlets 60
grilled scallops with
brown butter 82–3
hot and sour prawn
soup with lemon
grass 31
hot crab soufflés 57
Malayan prawn
laksa 29
marinated asparagus
and langoustine 77
mussels and clams and
lemon grass 79
paella croquettes 84
potted prawns 47
prawn and egg-knot
soup 30
prawn cocktail 76
prawn, egg and
avocado mousses 42
scallop-stuffed roast
peppers with pesto 81
scallops wrapped in
Parma ham 80
Thai-style seafood
pasties 71
tiger prawns with mint,
dill and lime 62
smoked fish and avocado
salad 105
smoked haddock pâté
39
smoked salmon and
haddock terrine 52–3
smoked salmon and rice
salad parcels 85
smoked salmon pâté 38

sole batons,
breaded 91
sour cherry soup,
Hungarian 23
Spanish garlic soup 14
spinach
Greek aubergine and
spinach pie 68–9
poached eggs
Florentine 111
spinach and rice
soup 21
spinach and tofu
soup 24
wilted spinach and
bacon salad 100
squid, fried 82–3
stuffed garlic mushrooms
with prosciutto 98

T
tartare sauce and crab
cakes 88–9
tarte Tatin, vegetable 66–7
Thai-style seafood
pasties 71
three-colour fish
kebabs 87
tiger prawns with mint,
dill and lime 62
tofu
hot-and-sour soup
28
spinach and tofu
soup 24
tomatoes
chilled tomato and
sweet pepper soup 11
fresh tomato soup 17
gazpacho with avocado

salsa 27
griddled tomatoes on
soda bread 65
panzanella salad 121
roasted tomato and
mozzarella salad 124–5
tomato and courgette
timbales 110
tricolour salad 123
tortellini chanterelle
broth 13
tricolour salad 123
turkey, juniper and
peppercorn terrine 54
twice-baked Gruyère
cheese and potato
soufflé 56

V
vegetable tarte Tatin
66–7
vegetable terrine,
grilled 48–9

W
watercress and orange
soup 25
watercress and pear
soup 12
whitebait, deep-
fried 93
wild mushroom and
fontina tarts 63
wild mushroom soup 16
wilted spinach and bacon
salad 100

Y
yogurt and cucumber
soup, cold 10